A VISUAL HISTORY OF COSTUME
The Seventeenth Century

VALERIE CUMMING

B T BATSFORD LTD, LONDON
DRAMA BOOK PUBLISHERS,
NEW YORK

Acknowledgments

ISBN 0 7134 4093 7

Typeset by Tek-Art Ltd West Wickham Kent
and printed in Great Britain by
Butler & Tanner Ltd
Frome, Somerset

for the publishers
B. T. Batsford Ltd
4 Fitzhardinge Street
London W1H 0AH

Published in USA by
Drama Book Publishers
821 Broadway
New York,   New York 10003

ISBN 0 89676 078 2

I would like to thank Aileen Ribeiro who suggested the
idea of costume picture books to Batsford, and then
allowed me the opportunity to prepare the volume on the
seventeenth century. My early interest in the dress of this
period developed under the guidance of Stella Newton
at the Courtauld Institute, and to her, and to Kay
Staniland, with whom I worked on surviving
seventeenth-century costume and textiles at the
Museum of London, I extend my gratitude for fostering
my interest in what was then a less-than-popular area of
English dress.

Many colleagues in museums and galleries have
provided useful information and fruitful discussions on
this subject in subsequent years, and recently I have been
patiently assisted by the publications officers of all the
institutions which provided illustrations. In particular I
would like to acknowledge the help of Celina Fox, Judith
Prendergast and Harry Matthews.

Olivia Bland, as always, provided invaluable
secretarial help and informed criticism of a less-than-
legible manuscript. My husband encouraged me
throughout this enterprise, and patiently ignored the
social isolation which my books seem to create for both
of us.

Lastly, but wholeheartedly, I want to thank Tim
Auger, Mimi Rolbant and Clare Sunderland of Batsford
who helped with editorial and pictorial problems, and
transformed a typescript with pictures into a coherent
and stylish book.

Acknowledgment of permission to reproduce the
individual illustrations is made in the List of
Illustrations.

Contents

Preface

A Visual History of Costume is a series devised for those who need reliable, easy-to-use reference material on the history of dress.

The central part of each book is a series of illustrations, in black-and-white and colour, taken from the time of the dress itself. They include oil paintings, engravings, woodcuts and line drawings. By the use of such material, the reader is given a clear idea of what was worn and how, without the distortions and loss of detail which modern drawings can occasionally entail.

Each picture is captioned in a consistent way, under the headings, where appropriate, 'Head', 'Body' and 'Accessories'; the clothes are not just described, but their significance explained. The reader will want to know whether a certain style was fashionable or unfashionable at a certain time, usual or unusual – such information is clearly and consistently laid out. The illustrations are arranged in date order, and the colour illustrations are numbered in sequence with the black-and-white, so that the processes of change can be clearly followed.

The pictures will be all the better appreciated if the reader has at least some basic overall impression of the broad developments in dress in the period concerned, and the Introduction is intended to provide this.

Technical terms have been kept to a reasonable minimum. Many readers will use these books for reference, rather than read them straight through from beginning to end. To explain every term each time it is used would have been hopelessly repetitive, and so a Glossary has been provided. Since the basic items of dress recur throughout the book, a conventional, full Index would have been equally repetitive; therefore the Glossary has been designed also to act as a selective Index; after each entry the reader will find the numbers of those illustrations which show important examples of the item concerned, and the earliest and latest example of each item.

List of Illustrations

Note The subject is followed by the artist, where known, then the medium, and then the collection. An Asterisk * indicates a colour illustration, to be found between pages 96 and 97.

19 **Anne Cecil, Countess of Stamford**
William Larkin, c. 1615
Oil on canvas
Suffolk Collection, Greater London Council

20 **Lady Dorothy Cary**
William Larkin, c. 1615
Oil on canvas
Suffolk Collection, Greater London Council

21 **Anne Wortley, later Lady Morton**
Manner of Paul van Somer, 1615 – 1616
Oil on canvas
The Tate Gallery, London

22 **Richard Sackville, 3rd Earl of Dorset**
Isaac Oliver, 1616
Miniature
Victoria & Albert Museum, London

23 **1st Earl of Monmouth and his family**
Attributed to Paul van Somer, c. 1617
Oil on canvas
National Portrait Gallery, London

24 **Charles, Prince of Wales**
Attributed to Abraham van Blijenberch,
1617 – 1618
Oil on canvas
National Portrait Gallery, London

25 *Unknown lady
Marcus Gheeraedts, 1618
Oil on canvas
Ferens Art Gallery, Hull

26 **2nd Earl of Arundel**
Daniel Mytens, 1618
Oil on canvas
National Portrait Gallery, London

27 **Countess of Arundel**
Daniel Mytens, 1618
Oil on canvas
National Portrait Gallery, London

28 **Lady Elizabeth Grey, Countess of Kent**
Paul van Somer, c. 1619
Oil on canvas
The Tate Gallery, London

29 **Lady Aston**
Attributed to Marcus Gheeraedts, c. 1619
Oil on canvas
The Tate Gallery, London

30 **Elizabeth Howard, Countess of Banbury**
Daniel Mytens, 1619 – 1620
Oil on canvas
Suffolk Collection, Greater London Council

31 **George Carew, Earl of Totnes**
After an unknown artist, 1619 – 1620
Oil on canvas
National Portrait Gallery, London

32 **Elizabeth, Countess of Southampton**
Unknown artist, c. 1622
Oil on canvas
National Portrait Gallery, London

33 **Lady Emily Howard**
School of Marcus Gheeraedts, 1623
Oil on canvas
Suffolk Collection, Greater London Council

34 **1st Duke of Hamilton as a youth**
Daniel Mytens, 1624
Oil on canvas
The Tate Gallery, London

35 **Lady Anne Carleton**
Studio of Michael Jansz van Miereveldt,
1624 – 1625
Oil on panel
National Portrait Gallery, London

36 **Sir Nathaniel Bacon**
Self portrait, 1624 – 1625
Oil on panel
National Portrait Gallery, London

37 **Called George Puleston**
John Souch, 1625-1627
Oil on panel
The Tate Gallery, London

38 **1st Earl of Carlisle**
Unknown artist, 1628
Oil on canvas
National Portrait Gallery, London

39 **Unknown couple**
Unknown artist, 1628
Oil on panel
Victoria & Albert Museum, London

40 **1st Duke of Buckingham and his family**
After Gerard Honthorst, 1628
Oil on canvas
National Portrait Gallery, London

41 **Unknown woman**
Cornelius Johnson, 1629
Oil on canvas
The Tate Gallery, London

42 **Unknown man**
Cornelius Johnson, 1629
Oil on canvas
The Tate Gallery, London

43 **The Needles Excellency**
James Taylor, 1631
Engraving
Victoria & Albert Museum, London

44 **Charles I**
Daniel Mytens, 1631
Oil on canvas
National Portrait Gallery, London

45 **Margaret Hallyday, Lady Hungerford**
Cornelius Johnson, 1631
Oil on panel
Suffolk Collection, Greater London Council

46 **1st Earl of Holland**
Studio of Daniel Mytens, 1632 – 1633
Oil on canvas
National Portrait Gallery, London

47***Queen Henrietta Maria**
Unknown artist, c. 1634
Oil on canvas
National Portrait Gallery, London

48 **French nobleman**
Unknown artist, 1634
Drawing, body colour
Victoria & Albert Museum, London

49 **Queen Henrietta Maria**
After Sir Anthony van Dyck, 1634 – 1635
Oil on canvas
Greater London Council

50 **2nd Earl of Warwick**
Studio of Daniel Mytens, 1635 – 1636
Oil on canvas
National Portrait Gallery, London

51 **William Style of Langley**
Unknown artist, 1636
Oil on canvas
The Tate Gallery, London

52 **Unknown woman**
After Sir Anthony van Dyck, 1636 – 1637
Oil on canvas
Victoria & Albert Museum, London

53 **Prince Rupert**
Studio of Sir Anthony van Dyck, c. 1637
Oil on canvas
Reproduced by courtesy of the Trustees,
The National Gallery, London

54 **Sir John Backhouse**
Unknown artist, signed V M, 1637
Oil on canvas
National Portrait Gallery, London

55 **Catherine Bruce, Countess of Dysart**
After Sir Anthony van Dyck, c. 1638
Oil on canvas
Victoria & Albert Museum, London

56 **Diana Cecil, Countess of Elgin**
Cornelius Johnson, 1638
Oil on canvas
Suffolk Collection, Greater London Council

57 **1st Earl of Elgin**
Cornelius Johnson, 1638
Oil on canvas
Suffolk Collection, Greater London Council

58 **Earl of Newport and Lord Goring**
After Sir Anthony van Dyck, 1638 – 1639
Oil on canvas
National Portrait Gallery, London

59 **A lady of the Spencer family**
Sir Anthony van Dyck, 1638 – 1639
Oil on canvas
The Tate Gallery, London

60 **An English lady**
Wenceslas Hollar, 1639
Engraving
Private Collection

61 **1st Baron Capel and his family**
Cornelius Johnson, 1639 – 1640
Oil on canvas
National Portrait Gallery, London

62 **Servant**
Wenceslas Hollar, 1640
Engraving
Batsford

63 **John Evelyn**
Hendrick van der Borcht, 1641
Oil on canvas
Private Collection on loan to the
National Portrait Gallery, London

64 **The Saltonstall family**
David des Granges, c. 1641
Oil on canvas
The Tate Gallery, London

65 **Elizabeth, Queen of Bohemia**
Gerard Honthorst, 1642
Oil on canvas
Reproduced by courtesy of the Trustees,
The National Gallery, London

66 **English gentlewoman**
Wenceslas Hollar, 1643
Engraving
Batsford

67 **English gentlewoman**
Wenceslas Hollar, 1643
Engraving
Private Collection

68 **Endymion Porter**
William Dobson, c. 1643
Oil on canvas
The Tate Gallery, London

69 **English noblewoman**
Wenceslas Hollar, 1644
Engraving
Batsford

70 **Cornelia Veth**
Cornelius Johnson, 1644
Oil on canvas
The Tate Gallery, London

71 **The Royal Exchange**
Wenceslas Hollar, 1644
Engraving
Museum of London

72 **Ballad Seller**
From *Chambers Book of Days*, 1644
Woodcut
Batsford

73 **Richard Neville**
William Dobson, c. 1644
Oil on canvas
National Portrait Gallery, London

74 **Mrs Hester Tradescant and her stepson John**
John de Critz the Younger, 1645
Oil on canvas
Ashmolean Museum, Oxford

75 **Sir Henry Gage**
Perhaps after William Dobson, c. 1645
Oil on canvas
National Portrait Gallery, London

76*3rd Viscount Fairfax of Emley and his wife**
Gerard Soest, c. 1646
Oil on canvas
National Portrait Gallery, London

77 **French gentleman**
Unknown artist, 1646
Drawing with wash
Victoria & Albert Museum, London

78 **English noblewoman**
Wenceslas Hollar, 1649
Batsford

79 **Mayor of London's wife**
Wenceslas Hollar, 1649
Engraving
Private Collection

80 **Merchant's wife**
Wenceslas Hollar, 1649
Engraving
Private Collection

81 **The execution of Charles I**
Unknown artist, c. 1649
Detail from a Dutch engraving

82 **2nd Duke of Hamilton**
After Adriaen Hanneman, 1650
Oil on canvas
National Portrait Gallery, London

83 **Elizabeth Murray, Countess of Dysart**
Sir Peter Lely, c. 1651
Oil on canvas
Victoria & Albert Museum, London

84 **Walter Strickland**
Pieter Nason, 1651
Oil on canvas
National Portrait Gallery, London

85 **Oliver St John**
Pieter Nason, 1651
Oil on canvas
National Portrait Gallery, London

86 **John Tradescant**
Attributed to Emmanuel de Critz, 1652
Oil on canvas
National Portrait Gallery, London

87 **Unknown woman**
Unknown artist, 1653
Oil on panel
Victoria & Albert Museum, London

88 **Thomas Chiffinch**
Attributed to Sebastien Bourdon, c. 1656
Oil on canvas
National Portrait Gallery, London

89 **Mrs Elizabeth Claypole**
John Michael Wright, 1658
Oil on panel
National Portrait Gallery, London

90 **Colonel the Honourable John Russell**
John Michael Wright, 1659
Oil on canvas
Victoria & Albert Museum, London

91 **Lady Jane Fisher**
Unknown artist, c. 1660
Oil on canvas
National Portrait Gallery, London

92 **Two ladies of the Lake family**
Sir Peter Lely, c. 1660
Oil on canvas
The Tate Gallery, London

93 *James, Duke of York
Sir Peter Lely, c. 1661
Oil on canvas
Scottish National Portrait Gallery, Edinburgh

94 **Charles II entering the City of London**
Dirck Stoop, 1661
Oil on canvas
Museum of London

95 **James, Duke of York**
Samuel Cooper, 1661
Miniature
Victora & Albert Museum, London

96 **Lady Castlemaine, later Duchess of Cleveland**
Samuel Cooper, 1664
Miniature
Victoria & Albert Museum

97 **Sir William Bruce**
John Michael Wright, c. 1664
Oil on canvas
Scottish National Portrait Gallery, Edinburgh

98 **9th Earl of Argyll and his countess**
Unknown artist, 1664 – 1665
Oil on canvas
National Portrait Gallery, London

99 **Queen Catherine of Braganza**
Attributed to Jacob Huysmans, c. 1664
Oil on canvas
Suffolk Collection, Greater London Council

100 **Sir John Harman**
After Sir Peter Lely, c. 1666
Oil on canvas
National Portrait Gallery, London

101 **Sir Norton Knatchbull**
By G. P. Harding after Samuel van Hoogstraaten, 1667
Drawing
National Portrait Gallery, London

102 **Unknown couple**
Unknown artist, c. 1667
Drawing and wash
Victoria & Albert Museum, London

103 **Lord David Hay**
David Scougall, c. 1667
Oil on canvas
Whereabouts unknown

104 **Mary Beale**
Self portrait, c. 1668
Oil on canvas
National Portrait Gallery, London

105 **Jane Monins, Lady Knatchbull**
John Michael Wright, c. 1669
Oil on canvas
Private Collection

106 **Figures** *à la Mode*
R. de Hoogh, c. 1670
Engraving
Victoria & Albert Museum, London

107 **William Legge**
After Jacob Huysmans, c. 1670
Oil on canvas
National Portrait Gallery, London

108 **Unknown woman**
Unknown artist, 1671
Miniature
Victoria & Albert Museum, London

109 **Thomas Sydserff**
John Michael Wright, c. 1672
Oil on canvas
Owned by the Church of Scotland Committee on Social Responsibility

110 **The family of Sir Robert Vyner**
John Michael Wright, 1673
Oil on canvas
In the Collection of Henry Vyner

111 *Habit de ville*
J. D. de St. Jean, 1673
Fashion plate
Private Collection

112 **2nd Viscount Brouncker**
After Sir Peter Lely?, c. 1673
Oil on canvas
National Portrait Gallery, London

113 **Duke and Duchess of Lauderdale**
Sir Peter Lely, c. 1674
Oil on canvas
Victoria & Albert Museum, London

114 **Mary of Modena, Duchess of York**
Sir Peter Lely, c. 1674
Oil on canvas
Suffolk Collection, Greater London Council

115 **The Baths at Bath**
T. Johnson, 1675
Engraving
By courtesy of the Trustees of the British Museum

116 **1st Earl of Bath**
John Michael Wright, 1676
Oil on canvas
In a Private Scottish Collection

117 *Habit de ville*
N. Bonnart, 1676
Fashion plate
Private Collection

118 **Charles II receiving a pineapple from Rose the gardener**
After N. Danckerts, c. 1676
Victoria and Albert Museum, London

119 *La dame de grand air*
N. Bonnart, 1677
Fashion plate
Private Collection

120 **Dame en habit de ville*
J. le Pautre, 1678
Fashion plate
Private Collection

121 *Homme de qualité en habit d'hiver*
J. D. de St. Jean, 1678
Fashion plate
Private Collection

122 *Dame en deshabille de ville*
J. le Pautre, 1678
Fashion plate
Private Collection

123 **Sir Leoline Jenkins**
Herbert Tuer, 1679
Oil on canvas
National Portrait Gallery, London

124 **Charles II and Queen Catherine**
Engraved frontispiece from Ogilby and Morgan's
Map of London, 1682
Museum of London

125 **Duchess of Portsmouth**
Pierre Mignard, 1682
Oil on canvas
National Portrait Gallery, London

126 **An English couple**
Engraving from *Description de l'Univers . . .*
Unknown artist, 1683
Victoria & Albert Museum, London

127 **Frost Fair on the Thames**
Unknown artist, 1684
Sketch plan
Museum of London

128 *Dame en escharpe*
N. Bonnart, 1685
Fahion plate
Private Collection

129 **Lady of quality**
Unknown artist, 1685 – 1686
Engraving
Private Collection

130 *Homme de qualité en habit d'espée*
Unknown artist, c. 1685
Fashion plate
Private Collection

131 **Coronation Procession of James II**
Engraving from Sandford's *History of the Coronation of James II*, 1686
Museum of London

132 **The Chariot of the Virgin Queen, Lord Mayor's Pageant**
Unknown artist, 1686
Pen, ink and wash
Museum of London

133 *Femme de qualité en habit d'esté*
N. Arnoult, 1687
Fashion plate
Private Collection

134 *Homme de qualité*
J. D. de St. Jean, 1687
Fashion plate
Private Collection

135 **Frances Stuart, Duchess of Richmond and Lennox**
William Wissing and Jan van der Vaart, 1687
Oil on canvas
National Portrait Gallery, London

136 *Dame de qualité à l'eglise*
G. Jollain, 1688
Fashion plate
Private Collection

137 **Arrival of Queen Mary of Modena in Calais**
Unknown artist, 1688
Detail from a Dutch engraving of the flight of James II
Museum of London

138 **The Squire of Alsatia**
Marcellus Laroon II, 1688
Engraving from Pierce Tempest's *Cries of London*
Museum of London

139 **Old Satten, Old Taffety or Velvet**
Marcellus Laroon II, 1688
Engraving from Tempest's *Cries of London*
Museum of London

140 **Old Cloaks, Suits or Coats**
Marcellus Laroon II, 1688
Engraving from Tempest's *Cries of London*
Museum of London

141*	*Homme de qualité garny de rubans*
J. D. de St. Jean, 1689
Fashion plate
Private Collection

142 *Femme de qualité allant incognito par la ville*
J. D. de St. Jean, 1689
Fashion plate
Batsford

143 **Robert Boyle,**
After Johann Kerseboom, 1689 – 1690
Oil on canvas
National Portrait Gallery, London

144 **Church of St Mary Overy, Southwark**
Unknown artist, 1689   1690
Detail from an engraving
Museum of London

145 **The Holbein Gate, Whitehall Palace**
Unknown artist, 1690 – 1692
Engraving
Museum of London

146 *Dame de la plus haute qualité*
J. D. de St. Jean, 1693
Fashion plate
Private Collection

147 *Homme de qualité en habit garny d'agrémens*
J. D. de St. Jean, 1693
Fashion plate
Victoria & Albert Museum, London

148*	**Marie Sophie Palatine, Reyne de Portugal**
Unknown artist, 1694
Fashion plate
Private Collection

149 **1st Earl of Halifax**
Sir Godfrey Kneller, 1693 – 1694
Oil on canvas
National Portrait Gallery, London

150 *Homme de qualité en habit de Teckeli*
J. D. de St. Jean, 1694
Fashion plate
Victoria and Albert Museum, London

151 *Femme de qualité en deshabille d'hyver*
J. D. de St. Jean, 1694
Fashion plate
Private Collection

152 **The Mercers' Chapel, Mercers Hall**
Unknown artist, c. 1695
Detail from an engraving
Museum of London

153 *Habit de cavalier*
J. Mariette, 1695
Fashion plate
Private Collection

154 **Prince James Stuart (the 'Old Pretender')
with his sister**
Nicholas de Largillière, 1695
Oil on canvas
National Portrait Gallery, London

155 **John Dryden**
James Maubert, 1696 – 1697
Oil on canvas
National Portrait Gallery, London

156 **6th Earl of Dorset**
Sir Godfrey Kneller, 1697
Oil on canvas
National Portrait Gallery, London

157 **Studies of head-dresses**
B. Picart, published 1703, drawn 1698 – 1701
Engraving
Private Collection

158 **Choir of St Paul's Cathedral**
Unknown artist, 1698 – 1700
Detail from engraving
Museum of London

Introduction

A visual survey of costume is bound to be subjective. It would be feasible, by searching assiduously through all the known visual sources, to provide dated images, one for each year of the century, eked out, within the allotted number of illustrations, by familiar or important pictures. This might give a spurious structure to this book but it would not confront the major problems with which costume historians work, nor would it provide an accurate reflection of the difficult spots in the century, when illustrations, which add some real strength to the understanding of the dress of the seventeenth century, are sparse in number or non-existent.

In the course of this introduction, which is divided into three sections, the problems, the visual evidence, and the costume, it should become clear to the reader that a definitive visual survey of seventeenth-century English costume would be difficult to provide in a book of this size. This book is therefore intended as an appreciation of seventeenth-century costume which will stimulate further exploration.

The problems
Dated illustrations containing clothed figures, whether portraits, engravings or drawings, can be more deceptive than those to which art historians examining the work of a particular artist ascribe a *circa* date. It is the role of the costume historian to analyse the clothed figures within the framework of knowledge about the vagaries and uncertainties which surround fashion and the artistic interpretation of dress. A painting dated 1665, for example, may be fraught with problems. Are the figures depicted in it fashionable city dwellers or provincial conservatives? Are they elderly, wearing a style of dress once fashionable which they cling to for sentimental reasons, or have they adopted a current fashion to fit this 'fly in amber' image of themselves? Are they young, rich, experimental? Are they from the lower orders in society, or do they practise a profession which dictates a certain style of dress which overlays or distorts a contemporary fashion? Or are they subscribing to an artistic and social admiration for a form of stylized dress, perhaps pseudo-classical or 'antique' or pastoral, which they and/or their chosen artist wish to translate into a timeless fashion, thus conveying to posterity their ability to transcend the ephemeral styles of a particular year, decade or era? These are some of the many problems which have to be faced, and they are discussed within their chronological context throughout this book.

However, in essence the majority of the pictures in this book show the changing fashions worn by wealthier, city-based members of society, although certain exceptions have been made. Personal adornment is one of the most immediate forms of communication. It is possible to admire, ridicule, modify, copy, accept or reject the style of dress of another person without knowing or speaking to him. Fashions changed relatively slowly in the seventeenth century, but examples are included to indicate how quickly new styles were assimilated at all social and age levels. This social digestion of fashion is perhaps easier for a twentieth-century observer to understand than another problem area, that of stylized artistic dress. Admiration for the classical and pastoral worlds, seemingly so far removed from the busy, complicated world in which fashionable men and women competed for attention, favour and patronage, was reflected in many seventeenth-century portraits. A timeless, 'other worldly' and intellectually satisfying personal image became popular. Van Dyck had begun the process in the 1630s by reducing details in his paintings, concentrating on shimmering, lyrical folds of material, rather than producing a literal copy on canvas of how his sitters really appeared. This process was continued and accelerated by Lely, Kneller and other major artists working in England from the 1640s onwards. Examples are included in this survey, placing sitters into their chronological context, for no matter how much the artist wished to omit the ephemeral elements of fashionable dress, the sitter never wholeheartedly co-operated. Hairstyles, jewellery, the fit of sleeve, these and other small details place each individual firmly into a particular period. Ironically, children who were treated in so many other ways like miniature adults, were subjected to stylised portraiture less frequently than their parents. So although this book includes few children, leaving the detailed study of seventeenth-century children's dress for others, some are included because they provide accurate evidence, on a small scale, of a fashion which their elders wore but preferred to discard when being recorded for posterity.

At certain points in the survey even the selective use of children as miniature models for adult fashion is not enough to provide a comprehensive survey of fashionable dress. There are difficult decades: in the seventeenth century the 1650s and the 1690s are particularly bare of useful illustrations. Little can be done about the 1650s, but what is provided creates an evolutionary link between the 1640s and the 1660s. By the 1690s, it is possible to refer to French fashion plates to fill some of the gaps. Such fashion plates began to appear in the 1670s and they are included because the post-Restoration English Court looked to France for styles in dress, supplies of materials and accessories even when prohibitions were imposed (Charles II banned the import of French lace in 1675) or when the country under William and Mary from 1688 onwards was politically in opposition to France.

The aim in the compilation of this book has been to ensure that the reader can understand what he or she is looking at. Describing costume is never easy, and a head-to-toe description can be tedious when repeated over 150 times. Certain aspects of dress or appearance, obvious to the eye and unequivocal in use or construction, are omitted or described only at a point when a change occurs and attention should be focused on that particular area of a garment or an accessory. The descriptions are written so that a minimum amount of reference to the Glossary is required. The vocabulary of costume history is as problematical as its illustrations. Words were coined to describe particular fashions, and the proliferation of novelties each with their own contemporary name, can, if the original names are used excessively, reduce short descriptions to arcane nonsense. Therefore only the essential seventeenth-century words are used, and those readers who wish to perfect their vocabulary in this area should consult the Bibliography which suggests a number of sources which concentrate more fully on the specialist terminology.

The visual evidence

One major source of illustrations for anyone interested in seventeenth-century costume is portraits. Painting in England during this century was primarily concerned with portraiture. There are exceptions to this, but portraits were the main stock-in-trade of all artists working in England, whether they were natives or visiting foreigners. Van Dyck, working for Charles I in the 1630s, introduced landscape backgrounds into English portraits, and Lely, working from the late 1640s, painted a number of sitters in pastoral settings, but the religious subjects, the landscapes and seascapes of Italy, Spain, Holland and the Spanish Netherlands were not subjects which the average English client required from an artist. Individual portraits, family groups and delicate miniatures were executed in profusion to meet the seemingly insatiable demand for personal images. By the middle of the century artists of stature had evolved from craftsmen into men of influence and social consequence. Alongside this evolution came the changed attitude towards the sitter's appearance which was mentioned earlier. Fortunately for the costume historian, within the social categories of those who could afford portraits and among the range of artists from influential Court painters to provintial journeymen, there were many artists and sitters who preferred to provide literal interpretations of contemporary fashions. The detailed observation of the cut of men's and women's clothes

included fine stitching, the pattern of silk or lace, the fold of a collar or cuff, the decoration of a shoe or a fan, and are testament to the provincial English sitter's delight in accurate personal portraiture.

There is no major work which discusses the subject of seventeenth-century English portraiture as a whole. The story has to be pieced together from the published catalogues on major artists and the general catalogues of British and foreign museum and art galleries. The majority of portraits included in this book are selected from major collections on view to the public, for black-and-white photographs are no substitute for the colour, scale and impact of the original paintings.

Other illustrative sources are woodcuts and engravings taken from books or broadsheets about topical events which captured the public's interest: the Gunpowder Plot, executions, a Frost Fair on the Thames. Such illustrations are often crudely executed but they capture the overall look of the participants and the line of their clothes if not the small details of individual appearance. Sophisticated engravings, often published in a series, provide more detailed information, although it is necessary to exercise caution over the publication date given by the printer. For example, engraved portraits of distinguished people were often copied from earlier paintings, or a series might be re-published with later additions and the entire contents given the second date. Pierce Tempest's *Cries of London* are usually described as published in 1711, the date of the second edition, but the first edition appeared in 1688, and the majority of engravings date from then. Other engravings record major events: coronation processions, the flight of James II and his queen to France, the arrival of William III. It is doubtful whether these are more than fleetingly accurate representations of the event, but the dress of the major personalities will accord with what was generally worn at the time, even if it may not be a correct record of a particular individual's style of dress.

This caveat also extends to the engravings of churches and houses which appeared towards the end of the century. Figures are often included in these, usually to indicate the scale of the building, but also to enliven the architectural precision of the overall design. Some of these tiny figures, when enlarged, provide evidence of how an artist, whose primary interest was in something quite different, viewed the lines, the exaggerations, the movement of particular styles of dress.

The individual statement about personal appearance is provided by portraits, and it is not difficult to assess which sitters were in the vanguard of fashion and which ones trailed behind. Curiosity about the fashions of other parts of England or of other countries could be partly satisfied by looking at recent paintings. Travellers and diplomats could provide first-hand descriptions and occasionally brought home examples of what was worn elsewhere; and in London foreign merchants, embassies and couriers wore the styles of their own countries. Wenceslas Hollar, the artist, who travelled widely, produced several series of engravings of English and

European female fashions. They were records rather than attempts to influence fashion, and caution should be exercised regarding their accuracy, as Hollar suffered from poor sight!

Later in the century, in Paris, a number of artists began to produce what we think of today as fashion plates: annual, sometimes seasonal, illustrations of new styles of dress for both men and women. These plates were hand-coloured and accompanied by a brief description of the types of dress. Given the frequency of their appearance and the number of artists involved, it may be assumed that they did not merely record fashion, but in alliance with tailors, sempstresses and milliners, suggested new styles or variants of existing fashions. Some of the plates include samples of material, carefully cut to fit within the outline of certain items of dress; other plates survive in several colour-ways. They are witty and well drawn but perhaps more akin to modern fashion photographs in glossy magazines than to styles of dress which were generally worn.

Lastly there are pencil-and-wash sketches, drawings and designs which include figures. They are not primarily fashion statements; they may have been intended for a variety of purposes. Within this category is an exquisite fan leaf of 1686, identified by the Lord Mayor's pageant triumphal car contained within it. At the time that it was executed it constituted a superior form of ephemera, an amusing novelty, a topical accessory.

However, fortunately for posterity the significant portraits and highly treasured miniatures, are balanced, complemented and extended by the wide range of illustrations on paper. These were comparatively inexpensive at the time, but they survive in large enough quantities to provide a variety of sources to which a costume historian can refer.

The costume

At the beginning of the seventeenth century the exaggerated and constricting fashions of the late Elizabethan period were still worn. Women were dressed in elongated, tightly boned bodices worn with wide, tilted-wheel farthingales which encased the lower halves of their bodies like enormous cages. Men wore padded doublets with distended 'peascod bellies', with either wide trunkhose and canions or with breeches. Distortion of the natural shape of the body was admired.

Throughout the century these distortions increased and decreased in turn; the emphasis shifted but always emphasized one area of the body at the expense of the others. As the exaggerated bulk around the hips of both sexes disappeared in the mid-to-late teens of the century, the waistline rose, creating an elongated line which, when married to the lustrous plain satins and discreet jewellery recorded by van Dyck in the 1630s, provided the Caroline elegance which was perhaps the essence of the most discreet period of English dress in the seventeenth century. Whether this discretion was genuine or the elliptical vision of a great artist can be judged when the more literal work of provincial painters is seen alongside that of van Dyck.

Menswear became tubular in silhouette in the 1640s and 1650s, a line broken by the busy surface decoration and billowing linen which accompanied it. Women's dress grew ever more rigid around the upper torso, and this dichotomy in style between the sexes prevailed until the mid-1680s. The easier, more relaxed style of menswear developed into the vest and tunic of the mid-1660s, settling down, after an experimental period, into the happy combination of coat and waistcoat worn with breeches. Women, however, in the words of Thomas Mace, 1676, were ' . . . so pent up by the straightness, and stiffness of the gown-shoulder-sleeves, that they could not so much as scratch their heads for the necessary remove of a biting louse; nor elevate their arms scarcely to feed themselves handsomely . . .'. Such discomfort was alleviated eventually by the introduction of the mantua, a gown which had evolved from the informal nightgown.

The easy, almost smock-like looseness of the early men's coat was replaced by a more fitted line in the late 1680s, with the coat skirts stiffened by inter-lining and the fullness arranged into pleats at both sides and centre-back. This increased width was matched in female dress by the emergence of a shallow bustle or hoop, placed under the petticoats to support the looped-up fullness of their mantua skirts. So, by the end of the century, a restrained rigidity of style was once more apparent in the dress of both sexes, preparing it for the developments of the eighteenth century.

The major changes in costume, throughout the century, were an exploitation of all the possible permutations of existing styles, and the gradual evolution of new fashions. Fashion does not change suddenly; it is not only hindsight which allows us to expect the vest and tunic to appear in the 1660s, and then to expect further evolution of these two garments into the waistcoat and coat. Doublets, breeches and the earlier trunkhose had developed in every possible way: lengthening, shortening, widening, becoming tighter or looser until ingenuity had been exhausted. The bulky petticoat breeches and billowing shirts of the early 1660s were ready for a longer, looser coat as a replacement for the short, box-like jacket which had evolved from the doublet. Similarly, women's dress had explored all of the variants which were possible based upon a bodice, a skirt and a petticoat, until the one-piece gown, belted at the waist and fitting smoothly but comfortably over stays and petticoat, seemed a natural development which complemented the easier, less constricting lines of menswear. Once established, these two basic styles were able, in the eighteenth century, to follow a fresh voyage of development and change.

When examining the visual evidence of costume it is the details which are often overlooked, although they frequently provide the clues which establish a close date. Hairstyles, head-dresses, hats, jewellery, collars, necklines, shirts, smocks, belts, sashes, gloves, fans, stockings and shoes all contribute information. If an illustration contains enough of these details they are as significant, in some instances more significant, than the type of costume worn by a sitter or group of sitters. The designs of brocaded silks, of lace, of embroidery and the small surface trimmings all contribute to understanding of the taste of a particular period, and make it possible to discern whether the costume is typical or unusual of the period to which an illustration belongs.

The first 25 years of the seventeenth-century demonstrated an almost childlike delight in contrasting pattern and applied decoration. A period of restraint followed, during which novelties were tempered by discretion until with the Restoration of the monarchy in 1660, a joyful exuberance, carefully controlled during the Commonwealth, erupted. Decoration overwhelmed all articles of dress once more, exciting the astonished ridicule which accompanied fashion throughout much of the century. John Evelyn's description of a young man of 1661 is typical of this derision: 'It was a fine silken fop which I spied the other day through Westminster-Hall, that had as much ribbon about him as would have plundered six shops, and set up twenty country pedlars: all his body was dressed like a maypole, or a Tom-a-Bedlam's cap.'

Decoration was important in a century when tailoring was relatively unsophisticated. Bedecking with ribbons, braids and lace, the extravagant use of collars, cravats and sleeve ruffles, the addition of small accessories like fans, muffs and walking sticks are understandable because attractive or interesting variants were easier to fabricate on a small scale. The production of these accessories was distributed amongst various specialist tradesmen, although the majority of the softer items, such as collars, cravats and ruffles were made by sempstresses who, by the end of the century, had evolved into mantua makers with a large new clientele of female customers. For the first 75 years of the century men's and women's outer garments were usually made by tailors, and even after the evolution of sempstresses into dressmakers (to use a modern term), tailors continued to make the more structural female garments such as stays and riding habits.

Both sexes wore identical materials and could choose from a range of colours which relied on natural dyes for their richness. Materials and trimmings were selected on visits to drapers, linen and silk merchants and milliners, so called because many small trimmings originally came from Milan. Imported materials were an expensive but integral element of fashionable dress. Silk materials, satin, velvet and brocade, were designed and woven in Italy and France, and many of the decorative trimmings, much of the lace and some accessories also came from these countries. Linen, used for shirts and smocks, was imported from the Netherlands and Germany early in the century, although a native industry grew up around Manchester in the second half of the century, using imported flax. England produced excellent wool cloth in a variety of grades and widths, but such cloth was not much worn by fashionable people until late in the century when it proved excellent material for men's coats.

Prohibited imports were few in the seventeenth century, although Charles II tried to ban both French and Flemish lace in 1675 (the Flemish lace was exempted when retaliation against English wool exports to the Netherlands was mooted). However, during the century the English ability for absorbing new ideas, newcomers and changed circumstances led to a broader-based native textile industry. Thriving linen and cotton industries using imported flax and yarn developed in the north of England; an embryonic luxury silk industry was established in Spitalfields by Huguenot refugees; and competent lace was being produced in South Devon and the East Midlands. The strength of these industries was constantly tested by the fashionable pursuit of exotic novelties, but by the end of the century there was a much wider choice of both English and imported goods than could have been foreseen in 1600.

London was the major shopping centre for anyone with pretensions to be a member of the fashionable world, but during the century, as other cities prospered, a wider range of shops appeared outside the capital. In 1699 Celia Fiennes was impressed on a visit to Newcastle because, 'Their shops are good and of distinct trades, not selling many things in one shop as is the custom in most country towns and cities.' There was a thriving secondhand market in both clothes and materials, more than occasionally fuelled by the many thefts of clothes which were regularly reported in the *London Gazette*. Clothes were a valuable commodity in an age when social position was usually associated with the ability to afford a fashionable wardrobe, and the judicious re-sale of rich garments could help payment of a large tailor's bill.

There were many variations of clothing in the wardrobe of a fashionable man or woman. Diaries, letters, accounts record expenditure on items of dress which were intended to suit many occasions, from the informality of private apartments through to the most magnificent Court occasions. Privately, both men and women could relax in informal loose gowns, worn over their shirts and breeches or over smock and stays. On semi-formal family occasions like weddings, christenings and funerals certain styles of dress were worn, and small accessories like gloves and scarves were presented to guests. There was no agreed colour for bridal wear in the seventeenth century, but a death and a period of mourning required black clothes, and this sombre colour might be worn by an elderly widow for the remainder of her life. Clothes for travelling and riding were essential elements in a complete wardrobe, and made use of the fine wool cloth at which the English excelled. At Court, the round of public ceremonies and private parties dictated fine clothes and magnificent jewellery, and courtiers spent a great deal of money on the newest materials, colours and styles of dress.

It was a century of restless exuberance, partly explained by the political upheavals, but also prompted by the increased travel and communication between countries. The English were fascinated by novelties, often adopting a foreign style, a new accessory simply because it was available, although this eagerness for change frequently mitigated against elegance. If the contemporary commentators are to be believed, the century saw one absurd fashion after another, exciting derision and ridicule from the balanced and sombre-minded 'average Englishman'. However, this is not a phenomenon just of the seventeenth century; it is a concomitant of all fashions throughout history. Those who believe that there are more important considerations than the minute details of personal appearance will always mock exquisitely dressed contemporaries. Fashion may be ephemeral nonsense, but it also humanizes the protagonists of periods other than our own, and reminds us that individuality will always be expressed in the most personal of our possessions, our clothing.

PLATES & CAPTIONS

1 Henry, 3rd Earl of Southampton, c. 1600

Unknown artist

Note The fashions of the late Elizabethan period produced wide shoulders and hips which enhanced a narrow waistline.

Head Long hair was unusual, although certain poetically and artistically inclined courtiers affected it.

Body A plain shirt collar is visible under a lace falling band. The doublet has deep shoulder wings and longer tabs usually associated with jerkins (see 4), and the last vestiges of a peascod belly. Stiffened trunkhose and knee-length canions are decorated with applied braid. Fashioned hose are pulled over the canions and held with ribbon garters.

Accessories The flat-heeled shoes usually had light cork soles. Gauntlet gloves, a belt and sword hanger are embroidered with popular flower and leaf motifs.

2 The Cholmondeley Sisters, 1600 – 1605
Unknown artist

Note This naive but literal depiction of female dress illustrates the fashionable distortion of the anatomy which was admired.

Head The hair is rolled back from the face and contained within heart-shaped caps, a motif continued by the wide, pleated linen halo ruffs pinned to the cap fronts. The shallow inner ruffs are worn as standing half-collars with inner borders of ruched linen.

Body Padded sleeves with wide upper arms and broad, ribbon-decorated shoulder wings increase the top-heaviness of the upper torso. Blackwork embroidery decorates the stiffened stomachers, and all of the lace edging is *en suite*.

Accessories The pearl, enamel and gemstone necklaces are typical of the inexpensive, delicate chains made by jewellers in this period.

3 Unknown woman, 1602
N. Hilliard

Note A young woman dressed in the fashions of the merchant class or country gentry.

Head The full hairstyle owes its bulk to a padded roll, and is emphasized by the gauze and lace wired cap. A shallow-brimmed, high-crowned hat is held in place by hat pins.

Body The full ruff is softening into a collar revealing the neck and throat. The dark, stiffened sleeves and edge of the bodice provide a frame for the softly fitted central bodice; above the blackwork embroidery the ruched linen smock is visible. The combination of ruching and pinking on the bodice is more typical of sixteenth-century dress.

Accessories The delicate chain necklace and flowers provide simple ornaments.

4 Sir Walter Ralegh and his son, 1602
Unknown artist

Note The early-seventeenth-century delight in decoration (pinking, embroidery, applied braid, and lace) are clearly evident in this double portrait.

Head Short hair worn with a neat moustache and spade beard was usual for mature men. The round-brimmed hat trimmed with an aigrette is tipped at a fashionable angle.

Body Shallow ruffs and falling bands were interchangeable, and are matched by appropriate cuffs. Sir Walter's jerkin is fastened only at the waist to display the doublet beneath. Shorter, rounder trunkhose are worn with plain canions, with the stockings rolled above the knee, held by tight garters. The younger Ralegh wears an alternative fashion of doublet and matching breeches.

Accessories The boy's gloves have embroidered tabs. Both father and son wear swords. Although Ralegh senior was a soldier the carrying of a sword is equally associated with gentlemanly rank, and is thus appropriate for a boy. This wearing of swords is found throughout the century.

5 Edward, 1st Baron Herbert of Cherbury, 1603 – 1605
Perhaps after I. Oliver

Note An informal portrait revealing small constructional details of dress.

Head Shoulder-length hair and small beards were often worn by younger men.

Body The inside of the shirt reveals the neckband and the attachment to it of the linen falling band, a type of collar. The matching cuffs complete a set of lace; these accessories were expensive, costing as much as £7 per set for imported lace at this date. The embroidered doublet, with tabbed shoulder wings, is partly masked by the shoulder cape, often worn in this manner across one side of the body (see 6).

CONCILIVM SEPTEM NOBILIVM ANGLORVMCONIVRANTIVM IN NECEM IACOBI ·
MAGNÆ BRITANNIÆ REGIS TOTIVSQ · ANGLICI CONVOCATI PARLEMENTI ·

Bates
Robert Winter
Christopher Wright
Iohn Wright
Thomas Percy
Guido Fawkes
Robert Catesby
Thomas Winter

6 The Gunpowder Plot Conspirators, 1605
Unknown artist

Note An informal group of men from the middle of the social spectrum.

Head All of the men have long hair, full over the ears, and both beards and moustaches. Their hats have crowns of various heights, but with wider, softer brims.

Body Plain, falling bands are open at the neck. Robert Winter's pose shows how the band needed to be supported on a metal support: a pickadil. The doublet and jerkins with contrasting sleeves may be of buff, much worn by military men. Both Winter and Catesby wear their capes over the right shoulder, holding its fullness folded back over the arm.

Accessories Bates wears a pendant earring, Winter a ring and several have imposing jewels in their hats.

22

7 Anne Vavasour, c. 1605
M. Ghccraedts

Note This style of dress was expected at Court. Queen Anne, like Queen Elizabeth, admired the formality of the farthingale.

Head An upswept, formal hairstyle, its structured braids elaborately decorated, marks a temporary elongation of the female appearance.

Body A small halo ruff sits between ornately trimmed shoulder wings. The stiffened bodice, worn over stays, has a more rounded decolletage. A wheel farthingale is worn under the skirt, its open front held by rosettes, but revealing something of the scallop-edged petticoat beneath. The gathered upper panel of the skirt is, in reality, a long basque from the bodice, blurring the edge of the farthingale.

Accessories Rich jewels, lavish and unusual embroidery, ribbons and lace trimmings, and the fan suspended at the waist, provide suitable embellishments for a formal style of dress.

8 James I & VI, c. 1605
J. de Critz

Note The conservative fashions of the mature man, but with suitable richness of decoration.

Head The hairstyle and hat, although the crown is higher and the jewel more splendid, echo fig. 4. The ties of the falling band are seen below the beard.

Body The lines of the doublet are easier, with shallower shoulder wings, narrow sleeves, shallow tabs and moderate padding at the waist. The points attaching doublet to the paned trunkhose are tied in bows at the waist. Short canions follow the line of the leg. The shoulder cape is fur-lined: a winter fashion of the wealthy.

Accessories Rich jewellery is in contrast to the plain gloves, which are functional rather than handsome.

23

9 Queen Anne, c. 1610
After M. Gheeraedts

Note A state portrait illustrating the richness, formality and over-decorated qualities of Jacobean female dress.

Head This soft, full, halo hairdressing was fashionable for about 10 years, and is complemented by a deep standing collar.

Body The false hanging sleeves extend the shoulder line, and the small waist is emphasized by the wide oval neckline and tip-tilted fullness of the farthingale; both bodice and skirt are made from Italian brocaded silk. The decolletage is masked by fine linen.

Accessories The exquisite and delicate lace, the ribbon favour on the arm, the feather fan and the lavish pearls and jewels are accessories of great formality.

10 Henry, Prince of Wales, c. 1610
R. Peake

Note The contemporary interest in noticeable display, in the form of unmatched pattern and decoration is well illustrated.

Head Short hair and smooth complexion were the marks of the very young man.

Body The standing collar frames the head revealing the straight shoulder line. The shoulder wings of the jerkin are so shallow that they allow the doublet shoulder wings to form a stepped effect from beneath. The short trunkhose are much fuller, almost oval in shape, but with long stockings and not canions.

Accessories The shoes have a shallow heel and are decorated with large, spangled rosettes. The hat and gloves are of the fashionable shape, made richer by the addition of jewelled trimmings.

11 Phineas Pett, c. 1612
Unknown Dutch artist

Note A skilful and successful shipbuilder, following the main trends of fashion but unable to afford its richest elements.

Head Over his short hair Pett is wearing a nightcap, an inappropriately named informal alternative to a hat. These were made from linen, richly embroidered and edged with lace and spangles.

Body The standing collar has a feature of decorative pleats which reduce the material to fit the neck; the matching cuffs are similarly made. The doublet is decorated with long slashes to reveal the lining material. The breeches are very full, padded with bombast to create a bulky silhouette.

Accessories The belt and sword hanger have embroidery similar, but not identical, to the braid on the breeches.

12 Edward Sackville, 4th Earl of Dorset, 1613
See colour plates, between pp. 96 and 97.

13 Queen Anne, 1612 – 1613
W. Larkin (attr.)

Note The Queen is dressed in mourning for her son, Henry, Prince of Wales.

Head The full hairstyle is arranged in softly curving waves, with a lock of hair brought over one shoulder. The method of supporting the cap is visible, but is both decorative and functional.

Body The deep decolletage is broken by the lace-edged ties of the full, tall-collared cloak. The quality and structure of the lace is very clear.

Accessories Both the pendant earrings and the jewelled brooch are appropriately sombre.

14 Richard Sackville, 3rd Earl of Dorset, 1613
W. Larkin

Note The painstaking care taken in achieving this appearance is matched only by its extraordinary brashness.

Head The short hairstyle is accompanied by a wispier beard and moustache, allowing more of the wide lace standing collar to be seen.

Body The doublet is close-fitting, but the matching gauntlet gloves are wide and deep, to cover but not crush the lace cuffs. The breeches are fuller at the lower edge, balancing the collar width. The cape is lined with shag, and the hat, in the background, has a matching band.

Accessories The garters are lavishly decorative. The clocks on the stockings contrast with all the other embroidery, but the shoes match the doublet and gloves.

15 Execution of Edmund Geninge, 1614
Unknown artist

Note This naive illustration is full of the small variations present in dress worn at any one time.

Head The majority of the figures are short-haired and bearded. They wear high-crowned hats, some with shallow, firm brims, others with full, soft brims.

Body Small standing collars and ruffs predominate. The older men, or those with an official function, wear ankle-length, fur-lined gowns; others wear capes of thigh or knee length. The doublets and jerkins are mainly accompanied by full breeches, but one man wears trunkhose.

Accessories Shoes are fairly flat, but a slightly raised heel can be seen on the right of the middle row of figures.

Vitæ norma decens pariter mors iunxerit Vna,
Hæc duo Thesea pectora nexa fide.

M. bas. f.

27

16 Mary, Lady Scudamore, 1614-1615
M. Gheeraedts

Note Informal dress was easily as rich in appearance as the formal dress worn by women, although more comfortable.

Head The hair, full at the sides, but flatter on the crown, allows the cap of wired linen and lace to fit forward over the head. Deep cuffs match the cap, but a plain ruff, with tasselled tie strings, creates a break between patterned cap and dress.

Body A full-length gown is worn loose, but its buttons and loops could fasten. The blackwork embroidery of the linen jacket has a sinuous design complemented by the bolder pattern on the petticoat.

Accessories The black ribbon bracelet is a use of ribbon found among much jewellery at this period. Plain gloves with contrasting cuffs were popular with men and women.

Marty 12
Anno Domini
1614

No Spring Till n

17 Dudley, 3rd Baron North, 1614 – 1615
Unknown artist

Note A glittering young courtier combining the elegance and brashness which characterized the fashionable world.

Head The softly waving, fuller hairstyle echoes that of women at this date.

Body The small, densely pleated ruff was still fashionable; the choice between styles of neckwear was left to individual taste. An embroidered jerkin with false hanging sleeves matches the stiff trunkhose worn with a plain doublet. Deep cuffs mirror the decoration and pleating of the ruff. The stockings are magnificently embroidered with rich clocks at both sides of each leg.

Accessories Low-heeled shoes are dwarfed by glittering rosettes of spangled ribbon. The hat, high-crowned, is a plain beaver.

18 Catherine Knevet, Countess of Suffolk, c. 1615
W. Larkin

Note One of the many styles of dress worn by fashionable women in this transitional period before the farthingale disappeared.

Head The hair is softer, drawn away from the sides of the face.

Body The high, tiered ruff stands away from the bodice emphasizing the wide shoulder line with its shoulder wings containing both main and hanging sleeves. The bodice has buttons and tabs like a man's doublet; below it a short, gathered basque echoes the bodice construction worn with a farthingale. The open-fronted skirt reveals a richly embroidered petticoat edged with metal lace.

Accessories The low-heeled shoes with glittering rosettes are similar to male footwear (see 17). A formal rope of pearls and narrow, deep cuffs reinforce the elongated but more naturalistic line.

19 Anne Cecil, Countess of Stamford, c. 1615
W. Larkin

Note An unusual use of material provides a focus of attention for another transitional fashion.

Head A smooth roll of hair gives depth to the head while the cut-work lace ruff provides a frame for the face.

Body Hanging sleeves billow out around the main sleeve, but are attached and turned back at the elbow to reveal the lining silk. The skirt has a flattering, natural line, but the smooth pattern of applied embroidery and slashing on the bodice and side skirts is given a three-dimensional quality on the hanging sleeves and central area of skirt by pattern realignment and extravagent use of material.

Accessories The ribbon bracelets (one attached to a ring), the pearl rope and plain fan appear secondary to the large, lace-edged handkerchief which is an accessory rather than a functional necessity.

20 Lady Dorothy Cary, c. 1615
W. Larkin

21 Anne Wortley, later Lady Morton, 1615 – 1616
Manner of P. van Somer

Note A warm gown, an informal jacket and petticoat are transformed by rich surface decoration into garments of exuberant grandeur.

Head A full hairstyle seems essential for this type of wired gauze cap, and is as effective with a standing collar of lace as with a plain ruff (see 16).

Body The way the gown is held across the body reveals its fullness and sinuous metal embroidery, but partly masks the embroidered linen jacket with a deep basque which is fastened by ribbon ties. The ankle-length satin petticoat allows the shoes to be seen to advantage. The deep cuffs make a feature of the use of two tiers of lace.

Accessories The only items of jewellery are pendant pearl earrings.

Note This type of formal Court dress prevailed throughout the lifetime of Queen Anne but looks rigid and clumsy beside other contemporary fashions.

Head The width of the hairstyle is dwarfed by the wired standing collar and deep ruff.

Body The fitted sleeves, with their decorative hanging panels, and the stiffened bodice create a frame for the low decolletage. The pleated and gathered basque and open-fronted skirt with petticoat below, worn over the farthingale, balance the shape of the standing collar.

Accessories The formal arrangement of pearls, as ropes, bracelets and individual decorations, contrasts with the delicate enamelled chain and thin silk ribbons worn round the neck, one wrist and in the ears.

22 Richard Sackville, 3rd Earl of Dorset, 1616
I. Oliver

Note An archetypal fashionable young courtier, whose interest in dress is a well-documented feature of his interests.

Head The hair is short, brushed upwards on the crown of the head; the beard and moustache are lighter and carefully groomed.

Body A shallower standing collar reduces the emphasis on the upper torso, as do the closely fitted doublet and sleeve with vertical braid decoration. The waistline is rising slightly to accommodate the growing bulk of the trunkhose; the embroidered panes of the trunkhose are matched, in a reduced version, by the belt and sword hanger. Embroidered clocks on the hose and substantial rosettes on the shoes draw attention to the lower legs and feet.

23 1st Earl of Monmouth and his family, c. 1617
P. van Somer (attr.)

Note A rare family group whose clothes reflect their personal tastes, and the variations imposed by income and age.

Head The similarity in the shape of the hairstyles of the younger men and the women are noticeable: moderately full, brushed away from the face; whereas the father prefers the shorter hair and spade beard of his youth.

Body All of the neckwear is different; from the left: a standing collar, a full ruff, a wide layered ruff unpinned at the front, a falling ruff, and a shallow layered ruff. The pose and sombre colouring allows only the younger men to be clearly seen. Their fitted doublets have higher waistlines and substantial tabs; full breeches are worn to just above the knee and shoulder capes fall over one arm. Spangled lace garters complement their shoe rosettes.

Accessories Jewellery is sparse: only earrings and the young woman's pearl head-dress. The earl holds his wand of office as Chamberlain to the Prince of Wales.

24 Charles, Prince of Wales, 1617 – 1618
A. van Blijenberch (attr.)

Note A restrained example of the evolving triangular outline of men's fashions.

Head Short hair and a smooth, beardless face are encompassed by a fashionable layered ruff which, in this instance, has points of similarity with the shoe rosettes.

Body The high-waisted doublet suits a young man's figure, as do the matching breeches. The brocaded silk has been slashed to enhance rather than detract from the sprig motifs, and the applied braid provides an elongation of line to balance the bulkiness of the lower torso. The fur-lined shoulder cape is pushed up the arm to reveal the delicate lace of the cuffs. The prince wears Garter orders.

25 Unknown lady, 1618
M. Gheeraedts

See colour plates, between pp. 96 and 97.

26 2nd Earl of Arundel, 1618
D. Mytens

Note A sombre style of dress reflecting the wearer's official role.

Head The hair is brushed back at the sides and upwards on the crown of the head and is worn with a neat moustache and pointed beard.

Body The layered ruff is of linen edged with lace. A full-length, fur-lined gown with short upper and long hanging sleeves is worn over plain dark doublet and breeches. The cuffs are plain linen, and the shoes are tied with the simplest of bows. The emphasis is placed on the earl's Garter orders, wand of office and collection of sculptures in the background.

27 Countess of Arundel, 1618
D. Mytens

Note An elegant foretaste of changes in women's dress which developed in the 1620s.

Head The hairstyle is a softer, more naturalistic version of the curled and waved style of the later Jacobean period.

Body A standing lace collar is widened, half-circular in form, and placed inside the bodice neckline. The low decolletage and rising waistline shorten the upper torso. The sleeves and front of the skirt, although the arrangement of folds creates a distorted view, are decorated with the tags associated with points on men's doublets. The layered lace cuffs are less conical and fit closer over the sleeve.

Accessories The fine array of jewellery includes a pearl coronet, earrings and pendant, ebony beads on the bodice neckline and substantial gemstone bracelets, ring, brooch, cross and hair ornament.

28 Lady Elizabeth Grey, Countess of Kent, c. 1619
P. van Somer

Note Queen Anne died in 1619 and this portrait is of one of her ladies in mourning dress. Black was not synonymous with mourning, but the details of dress are correct for mourning in this instance.

Head The hairdressing is of the formal, earlier style associated with Court dress and is surmounted by a small cap trimmed with feathers.

Body The standing ruff and deep, matching cuffs are also of the traditional size and construction. A high waistline draws extra attention to the low decolletage, but an elongated line is created by the additional length of skirt and the long, hanging over sleeves.

Accessories The ebony beads are held in position by ties on the shoulder and the central rosette. A signet ring is tied around one wrist by a silk ribbon point; the brooch on the left bosom contains the emblem of Queen Anne.

29 Lady Aston, c. 1619
M. Gheeraedts (attr.)

Note The late transitional phase of fashionable Jacobean female dress with a high waistline but no agreed style of collar or neckwear.

Head A rather straggling hairstyle, brushed over the ears, appears in the later Jacobean period; it is more naturalistic than seen in previous years, and appears curiously unkempt. A jewelled band with feathers adds height.

Body The small ruff stands high at the back of the head. The narrower, elongated line of the dress is emphasized by the higher waistline, relative lack of bulk in the skirt and long, pendant oversleeve. The regular geometrical design of the brocaded silk is usual at this date. Textile patterns changed fairly slowly, but faster than lace designs.

Accessories The delicate black jewellery is knotted silk or possibly small beads knotted onto silk.

30 Elizabeth Howard, Countess of Banbury, 1619 – 1620
D. Mytens

Note A restrained elegance characterizes the dress of this fashionable young aristocrat.

Head The straggling hairstyle is a curious contrast to the neat head-dress and embroidered linen ruff.

Body The dress is in two distinguishable layers: an embroidered jacket and petticoat worn under a tabbed jerkin with hanging sleeves and matching skirt. The two materials are similarly embroidered, and the use of a pale belt, decorative loops on the skirt and rosettes on the sleeves creates a harmonious unity between light and dark fabrics. The narrower line of the dress is heightened by the transparent gauze veil which is brought from the head-dress to the waist of the skirt.

Accessories A dark feather fan and white handkerchief continue the themes of contrasts, and the jewellery is a delicate mixture of pearls, gemstones and ribbon.

**31 George Carew, Earl of Totnes,
1619 – 1620**
After an unknown artist

Note A mature courtier, keeping in step with
fashion, but preferring the rich embroidery and
contrasting materials of his youth rather than the
more discreet ensembles of younger men.

Head The smooth short hair is worn with a
pointed beard and neat moustache.

Body A layered ruff is worn above a gorget: a
component of a suit of armour often depicted in
portraits of military men or those with military
aspirations. The high-waisted doublet is
balanced by its deep tabs. The paned trunkhose
are full, almost oval in shape, and lavishly
embroidered with metal thread. Layered cuffs
match the ruff, and knotted to the ruff ties, seen
under the gorget, is a ring.

32 Elizabeth, Countess of Southampton, c. 1622
Unknown artist

Body The layered ruff and deep cuffs are of
transparent embroidered gauze over linen. The
high-waisted bodice features panes of material
on the upper bosom and sleeves which display
the linen smock or a contrasting lining. The
continued practice of outlining seams and
binding edges with braid or ribbon add vertical
interest to a lightly patterned material.

Accessories The jewellery includes double
earrings, a rope of pearls with pendant monogram
jewel and miniature case, and a ring.

33 Lady Emily Howard, 1623
School of M. Gheeraedts

Note This awkwardly dark portrait contains
features of dress which not only look backwards
but also reflect current developments.

Head Lady Emily's hairstyle is neat and full
under its two-tier dark lace cap brought forward
over the brow, as in 32.

Body Behind the traditional full ruff (although
barely visible in this illustration) is a wide
standing collar of the same lace as the cap,
reaching at its widest to the bodice shoulder
wings. A sleeveless gown is worn over a bodice
and skirt. The bodice with tabs and a horizontal
waistline was equally as fashionable as the
shallow, pointed front. The plain material of all
of the garments is enlivened by slashing and
applied embroidery. Rings tucked into clothing
were worn as tokens of affection or
remembrance.

34 1st Duke of Hamilton as a youth, 1624
D. Mytens

Note A transitional style of men's dress which, although narrow in line, appears top-heavy and cumbersome.

Head Longer hair was newly fashionable for young courtiers.

Body The falling ruff is small, and matches the cuffs. A shoulder cape is worn over the doublet which has deep tabs and a purely decorative arrangement of ribbon points (doublet and hose were held together by hooks from the late teens of the century onwards). The shorter breeches almost have the appearance of softly gathered trunk-hose. The wrinkled stockings are only partly held up by the decorated ribbon garters.

Accessories The punched decoration on shoes was well-established and echoes the shape of the rosette. Plain gloves and a soft-brimmed beaver hat were usual accessories.

35 Lady Anne Carleton, 1624 – 1625
Studio of M. Jansz van Miereveldt

Note A formal array of jewellery, rich materials
and lace indicate the type of dress worn by a
mature woman at Court.

Head The simple hairstyle with its one loose
tendril is dramatized by the pearl band and
feather head-dress.

Body The standing collar is of a type seen
earlier (see 27), and is complemented by a deep
lace collar which masks the decolletage of the
bodice. The paned sleeves reveal a patterned
lining which adds to the richly decorated effect
created by the brocaded silk bodice trimmed
with metal braid.

Accessories Lady Anne's splendid array of
jewellery demonstrates the limitations of design
impose on jewellers before gemstone cutting
became more sophisticated.

36 Sir Nathaniel Bacon, 1624 – 1625
Self-portrait

Note A sophisticated country gentleman and renowned amateur artist, with fashionable tastes.

Head The longer hairstyle, brushed behind the ears, but shorter and fuller above the forehead, is worn with a carefully groomed, pointed beard and horizontal moustache.

Body The falling ruff is closer in style to a collar, although still layered like a ruff (see 34). Pinking and panes relieve the plain material of the doublet, and the vertical line of the appearance is enhanced by discreet tinsel braid. The panes on men's doublets invariably revealed their linen shirts rather than a contrasting material.

37 Called George Puleston, 1625 – 1627
J. Souch

Note A provincial sitter of some substance, aware of changing fashions, but adopting them more slowly, as his circumstances allow.

Head Shorter hair was worn by older men and those outside London, but the fashionable pointed beard and moustache were more readily adopted than longer hair.

Body The design of the lace on the falling band is painted with great clarity. Slashing, pinking and narrow braid relieve the simplicity of the doublet satin, and the stitches holding the shoulder wing tabs in line are clearly visible. The metal tags on the ribbon points, the weave of the check ribbons, the sleeve buttons, the arrangement of the cuffs and the embroidery and fastening of the belt are all revealed in some detail.

45

38 1st Earl of Carlisle, 1628
Unknown artist

Note The elegant, narrower line of men's dress in the late 1620s created a harmonious unity previously lacking.

Head The fuller, longer hairstyle favoured by the King but varying in length according to the age of the wearer (mature men were rather conservative), was established in fashionable circles, as were the pointed beard and moustache.

Body The wide standing collar, held by a pickadil, and long matching cuffs were less popular by this date. In the mid/late 1620s the waistline lengthened and the doublet tabs reduced in number forming a deep basque. Sleeve panes also lengthened revealing more shirt linen. The embroidery creates a harmony between doublet and breeches; the latter are longer, bulkier at the waist and hips but narrower at the knee.

Accessories The applied braid and fringe decoration on the gauntlet glove appeared in the late 1620s.

39 Unknown couple, 1628
Unknown artist

Note A provincial couple's dress reflects the time lag in adopting the latest fashions, and indicates the elements of change which were absorbed as being suitable for their status and social circumstances.

Head The hairstyles are simple. The man has adopted a pointed beard, but in a fuller form. The woman's hair is taken back from her face and into a roll which is covered with embroidered linen; the lace of her cap is *en suite* with her ruff, smock and cuffs. Broad-brimmed beaver hats were worn by many women of the merchant classes, or by country gentlewomen.

Body The man wears a falling ruff, and a short-sleeved, fur-edged gown over slashed doublet and breeches. The woman's ruff is a traditional round one. Although her bodice and skirt are plain they reflect the divergence between men's and women's waistlines at this date; women's remained higher.

40 1st Duke of Buckingham and his family, 1628
After G. Honthorst

Note An influential and wealthy family dressed in keeping with their
important role in the fashionable world.

Head The similarity between male and female hairstyles is apparent: long,
softly waving, full at the shoulder, although the duchess's has a slight fringe
and a knot of longer hair behind.

Body Her deep lace collar is wide over the shoulder with matching tiered
cuffs. The high-waisted bodice and skirt are of satin, embroidered in part
with spangles and metal thread, with a new style of sleeve: elbow-length
panes in two tiers held by ribbons. The duke wears a small falling band of
lace over a paned doublet with unusually long tabs, and matching breeches.
His fur-lined shoulder cape carries a Garter star.

Accessories The duchess's pearls set the mood for the simpler jewellery
which was fashionable from the 1620s.

41 Unknown woman, 1629
C. Johnson

Note This bust-length portrait of a country gentlewoman provides a detailed view of the new style of collar and sleeve.

Head The longer hairstyle is curled loosely round the face and over the forehead.

Body The detailed construction of the wide lace collar can be clearly seen, including the join between the narrower scallops of the neck edge and the larger-patterned lace of the main collar. The full panes of the sleeves, with ribbons holding the billowing material between the two tiers are emphasized.

Accessories Pearl decorations on the dress, in addition to a strand of pearls round the neck and pendant pearl earrings, were a feature of women's dress at this date.

42 Unknown man, 1629
C. Johnson

Note A fashionable young man wearing the longer, curling hairstyle always associated with the Caroline period.

Head The longer hair, with a fringe and with a curling lock asymmetrically longer over one shoulder, is worn with a wispy moustache.

Body The falling collar matches that worn by a woman in its depth and exuberant use of lace; it is tied at the front with tasselled cords. Plain satin was increasingly popular for men's and women's dress. Patterned textiles were worn but a growing restraint in the choice of material and decoration was a feature of the period from the late 1620s onwards.

THE NEEDLES EXCELLENCY
A New Booke wherin are diuers Admirable
Workes wrought with the Needle. Newly inuented and
cut in Copper for the pleasure and profit of the Industrious.

WISDOME   INDVSTRIE   FOLLIE

43 The Needles Excellency, 1631
J. Taylor

Note Taken from an earlier German illustration,
this scene affords a rare opportunity to see an
attempt at recording past and contemporary
fashions.

Body The figure on the left is dressed in the
manner of Queen Anne (see 9). On the right is a
figure wearing the fashions of the late teens or
early 1620s (see 27, 35). However the central,
seated figure, represented as industry, is
intended to appeal to domestic needlewomen,
such as wives and daughters of merchants and
country gentlemen; it is a crude but recognizably
accurate reflection of what was worn in 1628
(see 39). This style of dress would not have
changed dramatically over three years.

44 Charles I, 1631
D. Mytens

Note The King was the epitome of restrained masculine elegance, and his wardrobe accounts demonstrate a genuine interest in fashion.

Head The softly waving hair, longer at one side, is complemented by a pointed beard and an upward curling moustache.

Body The lace of the collar is a dominant feature, providing curving, sinuous lines in contrast to the elongated line of the doublet and breeches. A three-dimensional quality is given to the doublet by full sleeves, lines of metal braid and decorative points, matched by similar points at the knees of the moderately full breeches.

Accessories A glimpse of stocking is visible above the tightly fitting boots which are folded back into deep tops. The front flap of the boots afforded a handsome strap to which spurs were fastened.

45 Margaret Hallyday, Lady Hungerford, 1631
C. Johnson

Note A country gentlewoman, with London connections, dressed in her finest clothes.

Head Curling hair frames the face and a fringe curls over the forehead. A pearl head-dress holds a group of flowers to one side of the head.

Body A wired, standing collar edged with lace is combined with a wide collar over the bodice; the awkward assimilation of the patterned lace of each collar is seen on the outer shoulder. A fine linen partlet, attached to the smock, modestly covers the bosom. The ribbons restraining the panes and the ruffled lace cuffs enhance the decorative effect. The stomacher at the front of the bodice matches the embroidered sleeves, but the main bodice is plain.

Accessories The asymmetrical arrangement of jewellery was a feature of the time.

46 1st Earl of Holland, 1632 – 1633
Studio of D. Mytens

Note Various small but significant changes in men's fashions are recorded in this portrait.

Head The asymmetrical hairstyle invariably had the longer lock of hair falling over the left shoulder, partly masking the small collar.

Body The doublet has lost its tabs and has gained a deep basque, adding emphasis to the rising waistline. More shirt is revealed where the doublet is left unbuttoned. The breeches are longer and bulkier.

Accessories High-heeled boots with contrasting cuffs and boot tops draw attention to the lower leg. The wearing of overshoes with boots was briefly fashionable in the 1630s. The earl's gloves recall others of the 1620s (see 37) and his wide-brimmed hat was a universal men's fashion.

47 Queen Henrietta Maria, c. 1634
Unknown artist

See colour plates between pp. 96 and 97.

1635

Gentilhomme de la
suite de M de Noailles 1634

48 French nobleman, 1634
Unknown artist

Note The fashions of the French Court usually influenced the English, although after a time lag, and with some variations introduced by English tailors.

Head The hairstyle, beard, moustache and lace-edged collar would not have appeared out of place in England.

Body However, this style of doublet, beginning to take on the appearance of a short coat, casually unbuttoned, and with flamboyant rosettes, took longer to be accepted. The wide breeches with extravagant looped ribbons at the waist did not appear in this form in England until the 1640s.

Accessories The softly concertinaed leather boots with wide tops and lace linings appeared in England in the late 1630s, but the high-crowned, shallow-brimmed hat was not seen until the 1640s.

49 Queen Henrietta Maria, 1634 – 1635
After Sir A. van Dyck

Note The Queen wears hunting dress and is accompanied by her dwarf, whose dress is a perfect miniature of contemporary male fashions.

Head The full, softly curling hair with a lock arranged over one shoulder mirrors the male hairstyles of this date, as does the low-crowned, wide-brimmed hat and deep lace collar fastened at the neck.

Body The bodice collar is brought down to the waist and held by the looped belt. The bodice has deep side tabs and a central, stiffened stomacher. Skirt and bodice are of matching material which has been pinked. Narrow rows of braid create the impression of a narrower vertical line, although the skirt is full, worn over hip pads. The cuffs are of tightly gathered layers of linen.

50 2nd Earl of Warwick, 1635 – 1636
Studio of D. Mytens

Note A portrait containing elements of martial dress, leavened by fashionable features acceptable in non-military circles.

Head The relatively short hair of the older man is still worn with a lock of hair over the left shoulder.

Body A wide collar disguises the join of the breast-plate at the shoulder, but the long ties hang free. A sleeveless buff jerkin edged with metal braid is worn over the doublet. The patterned silk sash is tied in a full knot at the left side of the waist. The long, full breeches are tucked into close-fitting boots.

Accessories Plain leather gloves and a distinctly civilian walking stick are the only accessories.

51 William Style of Langley, 1636
Unknown artist

Note A sophisticated country gentleman dressed in keeping with the bulkier fashions of the mid-1630s.

Head As if to keep in step with the fuller, longer hairstyle of the later 1630s, the collar has gradually widened and grown in depth to hide the shoulders.

Body The bulkier sleeves, high waist and deep basque of the doublet are balanced by the breeches which are widening at the knee (see 48). The points at waist and knee have become stylized rosettes (see 48), and in order not to crush them the sword is suspended from a shoulder hanger, not a belt. All of the garments, including the cape on the chair, are of matching satin pinked and edged with narrow braid.

Accessories The accessories are plain gloves, soft boots with contrasting tops and lace boot-tops, a wide-brimmed hat and a walking stick.

52 Unknown woman, 1636 – 1637
After Sir A. van Dyck

Note A fashionable young woman wearing the lustrous satin and expensive, sophisticated lace which created a restrained elegance in women's dress.

Head The hairdressing is softer, pendant at the side of the head, rather than curled away from it, and the knot of hair behind is entwined with pearls and ribbons.

Body Although deep and wide in the usual manner, this collar illustrates another style of the 1630s which can be fastened modestly but still reveals some bosom; the matching cuffs are attached to the sleeve and fall forwards echoing the edge of the collar. The bodice fits the upper body and divides into deep tabs to accomodate the fullness of the high-waisted skirt.

Accessories The jewellery consists of fashionable pearls and two gemstone brooches.

53 Prince Rupert, c. 1637
Studio of Sir A. van Dyck

Note A young prince with both British and Continental European connexions, adapting his taste to suit the English Court.

Head Full curls, fashionably long, and no beard were worn by young men in their late teens.

Body A small collar, tied with a flourish of loops, reveals most of the gorget under which a buff jerkin is partly laced. The doublet is also open revealing the shirt. The decorative buttons and loops on the doublet front and open sleeves could be fastened if required. The sleeves have a contrasting turn-back cuff. Long, looser breeches are similarly decorated and have discreet ribbon loops at the waist.

Accessories The soft boots are developing the baggy creases and full tops of the European fashion (see 48).

54 Sir John Backhouse, 1637
Unknown artist, signed V.M.

Note A sombre study of a successful merchant.

Head A short hairstyle was preferred by many men outside Court circles, although they adopted the pointed beard and turned-up moustache worn with the longer hair.

Body The plain linen collar is of the shape and size worn at the item, but undecorated except for the knotted tassels on the ties; the matching cuffs are also devoid of decoration. The dark doublet, breeches and cape seem to merge together, but the high waistline is marked by a band of ruched loops created from the traditional points (just visible in the very dark original painting).

55 Catherine Bruce, Countess of Dysart, c. 1638
After Sir A. van Dyck

Note A partly accurate, partly stylized form of dress hinting at classical draperies, which appeared in the 1630s and causes confusion for costume historians, intermittently, for the rest of the century.

Head Soft ringlets became fashionable as the shape of the hairdressing moved towards extra length at the sides of the head.

Body The low decolletage, with no collar to modify it, was typical of this pastoral/classical style of depiction. The drapery sleeves are held to the bodice with brooches, but the emphasis is on the soft billows of silk, which have little to do with fashionable appearance. The lavish use of material, with the play of light and shade on silken folds, was intended to create a sense of timeless informality, but the hairdressing and waistline place the countess in the late 1630s.

**56 Diana Cecil,
Countess of Elgin,
1638**
C. Johnson

Note A realistic
representation of the
dress of the late 1630s
with its changing
neckline and soft,
bulky silhouette.

Head The curling
hair is long and full,
and is decorated with
flowers.

Body The squarer-
shaped neckline of the
late 1630s is
emphasized by the
gauze collar, cut low
across the bosom and
revealing the smock.
The smock sleeves are
rolled up below the
full, gathered cuffs.
Ribbons across the
bodice front hold the
stomacher and side
panels of the bodice in
place. The long skirt
trails on the ground in
a manner
characteristic of the
1630s.

Accessories A
charming painted fan
is held open to show
the flora and fauna of
its decoration.

57 1st Earl of Elgin, 1638
C. Johnson

Note The darkness of the dress emphasizes the narrow, elongated line of men's fashions at this date.

Head The shoulder-length hair is all one length, but worn with a slight fringe.

Body A deep lace collar and matching cuffs are foils to the dark, paned doublet, breeches and cape, all of which are edged with black lace. The breeches are somewhat narrower than the fashion.

Accessories The shoes have much sturdier heels, a development of the mid/late 1630s. The gloves have the black gauntlets associated with mourning, and the broad-trimmed hat still has a shallow crown.

58 Earl of Newport (left) and Lord Goring, 1638 – 1639
After Sir A. van Dyck

Note A softer, more informal style of dress contrasts with the severity of the armour worn by these two men.

Head The shorter, less full hairstyles (see 57) seem appropriate with the martial breast-plates.

Body Both men wear small collars, although Lord Newport's is an improvisation, with a wider collar pulled closer into the neck and pinned into an impromptu ruffled cravat. The sleeves are full with cuffs turned well back above the shirt sleeves, a style made possible, as Lord Goring's sleeve illustrates, by partial unbuttoning of the sleeve. Buff jerkins, shorter in length than before, are worn over satin doublets, and both men wear the loosely knotted silk sashes which were worn with armour.

59 A lady of the Spencer family, 1638 – 1639
Sir A. van Dyck

Note A typical example of the restrained elegance of women's dress in the late 1630s.

Head The loosely arranged, softer hairdressing diminishes the importance of the head, placing emphasis on the wide expanse of bosom.

Body Bands of lace edge the bodice and a glimpse of smock is seen over each shoulder, mirrored by the rolled-up sleeves glimpsed beneath the deep, pendant lace cuffs. The bodice is in one section, laced at the back, although the stomacher point appears at the front as an additional tab.

Accessories The jewellery consists of the usual earrings, necklace and bracelets of pearls.

60 An English lady, 1639
W. Hollar

Note A fascinating example of the way a famous engraver found his source material in the work of another artist (see 59), but subtly altered it. Hollar's work is of great importance in the 1640s as he was one of the few artists who was interested in variations of dress.

Body It is worth noting that although he apparently only reverses the figure from looking left to looking right, he also moved the sash bow to the opposite side of the waist where it could be more clearly seen, and he turned the smock edges at the neckline into part of the collar. Such variants may have existed, but any copyist, even Hollar, should always be regarded with some caution when details of dress are involved.

61 1st Baron Capel and his family, 1639 – 1640
C. Johnson

Note A detailed family group in which all of the children, with the
exception of the two youngest, are dressed as miniature adults.

Head Lord Capel's hairstyle and dress recall the portrait of Lord Elgin
(see 57) and Lady Capel's hair is formally curled but closer to the head.

Body His collar has less depth, and more linen is seen, but the dark
doublet and breeches trimmed with matching lace are very similar to Lord
Elgin's, although the sleeves are of a different design. The unbuttoned
doublet was a feature of the 1640s. Her linen-and-lace collar is a square,
folded to display two depths of lace, and pinned at the throat. Her bodice is
identical, in every detail, to those of her daughters. The stomacher is
separate, held by ribbon lacing.

62 Servant, 1640
W. Hollar

Note One of Hollar's invaluable illustrations which record other dresses in society apart from the rich and fashionable.

Head The hair loops round the ears and under a lace-edged hood which has been loosely rolled and pinned up on the top of the head.

Body A plain square, folded into a triangular shawl, is worn over the shoulders. The side view affords evidence of the fullness of the sleeves, and the deep basque of the bodice above the hip pads which are worn under the skirt and petticoat.

Accessories Over low-heeled shoes are pattens: a type of wooden-soled overshoe with an iron ring at the base to raise the wearer above the mud and filth of the streets.

63 John Evelyn, 1641
H. van der Borcht

Note The young scholar is rather provincial and old-fashioned in his style of dress.

Head The hairstyle retains the asymmetrical fashion of the 1630s.

Body The collar is in keeping with the smaller size which appeared as the sleeves became fuller. The billowing display of shirt linen was retained with the new fashions but the panes on the upper part of the doublet and the sleeves were being superseded by one open seam on the sleeve and an unpaned doublet body, left unbuttoned.

Accessories Plain leather gloves were always appropriate.

64 The Saltonstall family, c. 1641
D. des Granges

Note A provincial family group with money to spend on good clothes, but not in step with the newest fashions.

Head The seated women is dressed similarly to Lady Capel (see 61) but her hairstyle lacks a fringe. The man wears the newly fashionable high-crowned hat over his shoulder-length hair, and is clean-shaven.

Body His collar is of a moderate size, with the narrowest of lace edging. The high waistline of the open-fronted doublet and the fuller sleeves follow the fashionable line, but the breeches are not so full and short as would be seen in London.

Accessories The shoes are tied with a ribbon rather than a rosette, a change of the 1640s.

65 Elizabeth, Queen of Bohemia, 1642
G. Honthorst

Note A sombre illustration of the emerging line of fashionable dress in the 1640s.

Head The hair is smooth at the temples and the longer side hair falls in loose curls, with the knot on the back of the head.

Body The neckline is rounder, closely mirrored by the curve of the deep lace collar. The waistline is longer, terminating in a substantial boned peak which pushes the fullness of the skirt to the sides and back of the waist. The sleeves are less bulky, and a type of turned-back cuff is appearing, pinned back over the rolled-up smock sleeve.

Accessories Pearl and gemstone jewellery retains its importance but is discreet in its size and quantity.

Queen of Bohemia.

English Gentlewoman

M. Hollar fecit

Mulier Generosa Anglica, 8

66 English gentlewoman, 1643
W. Hollar

Note A rare illustration of a woman of substance, but not of the most fashionable circles, dressed in outdoor clothes.

Head A plain hood covers nearly all the hair.

Body A kerchief over the shoulders almost totally obscures the triangular collar, fastened at the neck, which is worn over the bodice. Narrower sleeves are edged with plain linen cuffs, and a moderately full skirt is seen under the linen apron, which is decorative rather than practical.

Accessories The small feather fan and the smoothly fitting gloves indicate social status.

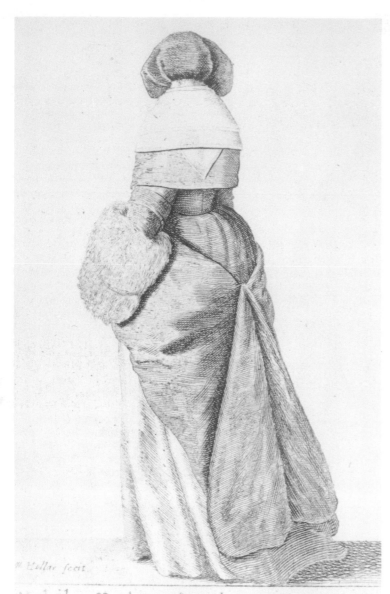

Nobilis Mulier Anglica

67 English gentlewoman, 1643
W. Hollar

Note An interesting back view of the style of outdoor dress worn in winter by moderately wealthy women.

Head The style of hood seen in fig. 66 is seen from behind, with tendrils of hair escaping onto the neck.

Body A plain linen square is folded into a triangular collar worn over a warm kerchief. The natural waistline and the double sleeves were new features of the mid-1640s. The open-fronted skirt is arranged carefully behind with a pin or clasp, providing a type of bustle which allowed ease of movement as well as revealing the petticoat.

Accessories Large muffs were popular winter accessories amongst those who could afford them.

68 Endymion Porter, c. 1643
W. Dobson

Note The fuller line of the 1640s is broken by billows of linen and ruffles of lace and ribbon.

Head The shoulder-length hair is now rather tousled, as if perpetually windswept, but the small beard and moustache are neatly groomed.

Body The collar could have been worn in the 1630s, but the unstarched cuffs are typical of the 1640s. The high-waisted doublet, with its deep basque, has fewer buttons, allowing a ruffle of lace on the shirt front to assume prominence alongside the ribbon loops at the top of the breeches. The full cape is so bulky that it is probably knee-length.

**69 English
noblewoman, 1644**
W. Hollar

Note The dress of
the mid-1640s has
evolved a line which is
distinctive but retains
some 1630s features.

Head The
hairdressing recalls
the style worn by
Elizabeth of Bohemia
(see 65), but the dress
is more modest.

Body A square
kerchief, folded
triangularly, but
shallower than earlier
ones, is worn above a
square-necked bodice
with a long, stiffened
stomacher. The two-
tier sleeves have
shallow, horizontal
cuffs above gloved
hands. The softer, less
bulky skirt is looped
back to reveal a
scallop-edged
petticoat.

English Gentle-
Woman

W: Hollar fecit 1644

Mulier Generofa Anglica.

9

70 Cornelia Veth, 1644
C. Johnson

Note Gentlewomen enlivened their plain dress by indulging in a prodigal use of lace and jewellery.

Head The hairstyle of the early/mid 1640s teased the hair softly onto the face, a style particularly flattering to the more mature woman.

Body A broad linen and lace collar, fastened at the front and extending to the outer shoulder, is worn under a loosely held square kerchief, folded triangularly. The bodice is plain, and high-waisted, with double-tier sleeves and shallow, gauntlet shaped cuffs.

Accessories The bodice provides foils for a discreet but impressive array of pearl and gemstone jewellery.

71 The Royal Exchange, 1644
W. Hollar

Note A mixed group of merchants, foreigners and fashionable men, congregated in an important commercial area of London.

Head The majority of men wore hats out-of-doors, ranging from the traditional wide-brimmed, low-crowned beaver, to the newly fashionable high-crowned hat with narrow, curling brim.

Body Various styles of collar are worn, either plain linen or lace-edged, and a few ruffs are seen, worn by older men. Cloaks of varying length are worn across the shoulders or casually wrapped over one arm. Most men still wear buttoned doublets with breeches, but second from the right can be seen the new style of short jacket and full breeches. Open-topped boots seem to be more fashionable than shoes. The ballad seller, to the left, is dressed rather like the servant (see 62) with the additions of wide-brimmed hat and apron.

72 Ballad Seller, from *Chambers Book of Days,* **1644**

Note The re-use of images, recorded earlier in Hollar's use of a van Dyck portrait, is continued by a broadsheet illustrator who copied Hollar. This crude figure, copied from the Royal Exchange (71) wears the modest dress of the humbler women in society.

Body A wide-brimmed hat, plain kerchief and cuffs, simple bodice with a deep basque, a moderately full skirt and apron recall the appearance of the servant of 1640 (see 62). In this instance such simplicity of dress reflects social circumstances, but it also indicates the style of dress worn by Puritans, adopted to show their disdain of worldly splendour.

73 Richard Neville c. 1644
W. Dobson

Note The ever-present symbols of warfare of the 1640s are softened by certain fashionable elements of dress.

Head The windswept hairstyle is accompanied by a smudge of hair below the bottom lip and a downward-curving moustache.

Body The neckwear is of interest: apparently a roll of linen, like a cravat, held within a soft, plain collar decorated with a loosely tied knot of black ribbons falling over the breast-plate. A buff jerkin is worn over a doublet with full sleeves, from which a swathe of shirt sleeve and plain cuff emerge. The coloured silk sash was an important means of identification in the Civil War, differentiating the wearers and their allegiances on the battlefield.

74 Mrs Hester Tradescant and her stepson John, 1645
J. de Critz the Younger 1645

Note The provincial simplicity of dress in the mid-1640s was not without fashionable features.

Head Mrs Tradescant's demure cap allows tendrils of hair to escape onto the face. Her high-crowned beaver hat is held in place by a band which passes under the edge of her cap and ties under the chin.

Body The bodice, partly obscured by the kerchief, has the new style of elongated front, with decorative laces, and the skirt is worn over the bodice side tabs, but the sleeves are fuller than the current fashion. The skirt could be looped back over an embroidered linen petticoat intended for show. The boy's doublet/jacket and breeches are simpler, miniature versions of the bulky dress worn by men.

75 Sir Henry Gage, c. 1645
Perhaps after W. Dobson

Note The contrast between the exigencies of warfare and the rich dress of many of its combatants was a feature of the Civil War period.

Head The hairdressing is neater and fuller than before, bushing away from the sides of the head and from under the small, informal skull cap.

Body A small linen collar is tied with a lavishly tasselled pair of strings. The doublet sleeves are very full, allowing the linen shirt sleeves to be pulled out from, and also below the turned-back cuffs. The richness of the doublet sleeves are a noticeable contrast to the plain buff jerkin enlivened only by the gilded laces suspended below the breast-plate. The full breeches have decorated side seams.

76 3rd Viscount Fairfax of Emley and his wife, c. 1646
G. Soest

See colour plates, between pp. 96 and 97.

77 French gentleman, 1646
Unknown artist

Note A similar style of dress was caricatured in a broadsheet cartoon of a London fop issued a year earlier.

Head A high-crowned beaver with moderate brim is worn over long, curling hair and accompanied by a tiny smudge of beard and a moustache.

Body A full, deep-collared cape is slung loosely over a doublet now reduced to a short, box-like jacket, open-fronted and sleeved to display the linen shirt. The breeches are short and tubular, decorated with lavish loops of ribbon.

Accessories The soft leather boots have wide tops, echoing the curve of the hat brim, and frothing with lace boot-tops.

80

78 English noblewoman, 1649
W. Hollar

Note A narrower, more elongated style of dress emerged for women at the end of the 1640s, with fullness concentrated at the back of the figure.

Head Smooth top hair and pendant ringlets are balanced by a full top knot.

Body The low decolletage is edged by a lace collar, deeper over the shoulders, fitting around the neckline rather than masking it. The stomacher is long and laced, with additional bones increasing the rigidity, on each side of the bodice. The two tiers of sleeve are differentiated, between a short, fitted upper sleeve and full, paned lower section. The scallop-edged skirt has all of its fullness taken to the sides and back of the waist.

Accessories Leather gloves, a fan and pearl jewellery complete the appearance.

79 Mayor of London's wife, 1649
W. Hollar

Note Only the wealthiest and most prominent London merchants became Mayor; his wife's dress reflects both wealth and social propriety.

Head The hair is taken back smoothly over the ears under the curving brim of the high-crowned beaver hat.

Body The survival of the deep-tiered ruff and cuffs amongst the merchant classes demonstrate a conservative grandeur similar to that of the Regent class in Holland. A wide curving collar, not clearly observed, and rather sketchily drawn, is in keeping with the styles of the late 1640s, as are the boned bodice with long-fronted stomacher, and double-tier sleeves. The skirt is looped back to display a fine petticoat.

Ein gemeine Burgers oder handwerck: mens Weib zu Londen,

Ciuis vel Artificis Londinensis Vxor.

80 Merchant's wife, 1649
W. Hollar

Note Subtle distinctions in dress between social classes were carefully observed in the seventeenth century.

Head The smooth hairstyle and deep-brimmed hat are similar to those worn by the Lord Mayor's wife (79).

Body A plain linen kerchief is worn over the shoulders and fastened at the throat. Much of the bodice is masked, but the sleeves are in one piece, fairly full, with plain cuffs. These and the embroidered petticoat revealed by the looped-up skirt but partly hidden by the apron, recall the dress of Mrs Tradescant (74).

Accessories The high-heeled shoes are trimmed with modest rosettes.

81 The execution of Charles I (detail from a Dutch engraving), c. 1649
Unknown artist

Note This rather grim scene provides evidence of the dress of ordinary London citizens in the late 1640s.

Head Headwear varies between skull caps and high-crowned hats with shallow brims, some with ribbon bands, others with jaunty feathers; all are worn over straggling shoulder-length hair.

Body There are varied forms of dress, with some men in deep-collared capes, others in jerkins and doublets with full breeches. The woman wears the style of dress depicted by Hollar (80). The executioner on the right, holding the King's head, and the royal servant, second from the left, wear fashionable loose fitting, tubular breeches.

Accessories In the foreground, the men wear low-heeled shoes with simple tie fastenings, but the platform group mostly prefer wide-topped boots.

83 Elizabeth Murray, Countess of Dysart, c. 1651
Sir P. Lely

Note An early example of one of Lely's many female portraits which simplify and distort fashion to create a supposedly timeless pastoral or classical informality.

Head The hairstyle is now softer, less obviously curled and arranged.

Body The bodice is dominated by large 'classical' sleeves, an artistic convention, with a scarf tucked carelessly under the arms. An edge of the linen smock falls over the bodice, which has lost its smooth, flat-fronted elegance, by the removal of the stays, and the pinning together of the front sections with jewelled clasps. Such informality might have been seen in the privacy of the home, but was not seen in fashionable society.

Accessories The jewellery is the conventional mixture of pearls and gemstones.

82 2nd Duke of Hamilton, 1650
After A. Hanneman

Note A dark, elusive portrait in which the Garter orders predominate, but it also provides other small details of fashion.

Head The hair, parted in the middle, is longer over the shoulders, but still rather straggling and lacking a distinctive style. The beard is a mere wisp and the moustache has dwindled into a thin line.

Body A small, plain linen collar is tied with heavily tasselled strings. Under the deep-collared shoulder cape the doublet sleeves are fuller and shorter, allowing the shirt sleeves edged with discreet plain ruffles to be displayed.

Elizabeth Murray,
Countess of Dysart

84 Walter Strickland, 1651
P. Nason

Note The severely vertical appearance of menswear increased in the 1650s as the traditional doublet and breeches changed in form.

Head The hair is shoulder-length but shorter on the top of the head.

Body The collar is smaller with the emphasis on the decoratively tasselled strings rather than the discreet lace. The cape masks much of the body, but cannot disguise the boxy, less- fitted line of the short brocaded silk doublet with its full, open sleeves. The tubular line is continued by the wide breeches, edged with deep loops of ribbon.

Accessories The high-crowned hat has a shallow brim, and the gloves are decorated with applied braid, bows and fringe. The unnaturally long-fronted shoes have a distinctive V-shaped break at the un-used toe.

85 Oliver St John, 1651
P. Nason

Note Sobriety of tone is lightened by an interest in fashionable fripperies.

Head There are inevitable similarities between this portrait and that of Walter Strickland (84), but the older St John has carefully groomed hair, a small beard and moustache.

Body His doublet is more traditional, the sleeves edged with crisp double-tier lace cuffs. The lining of his cape matches the doublet, but the breeches are even wider than Strickland's, decorated with braided button fastenings and ribbons.

Accessories Matching ribbons add interest to his hat and gloves. The soft boots have elongated toes and high, sloping heels, and the boot tops use both swathes of silk and lace to provide width to the lower leg.

86 John Tradescant, 1652
E. de Critz (attr.)

Note An informal portrait of the distinguished gardener who is seemingly uninterested in changing fashions.

Head The full, thick hair, just on the shoulders, and the pointed beard and moustache owe little to fashion.

Body A loose cape is pulled across the body. The full linen shirt with its attached collar, soft cuffs and narrow lace edging are in pace with newer styles. Separate collars and cuffs of fine linen and lace were worn alongside this type of shirt, but the ease and convenience of this style must have suited many men of greater consequence than Tradescant.

87 Unknown woman, 1653
Unknown artist

Note The rigid line of the bodice was softened by fuller sleeves in the 1650s.

Head The curls and ringlets are becoming wider and fuller at the sides of the head, whilst the knot is slipping down from the crown of the head.

Body The full sleeves, pinned to the bodice with brooches, owe something to the artistic conventions (see 83), but sleeves were increasing in size in the 1650s. The bodice is straight and long, worn over stays and laced at the back, and the simple swathe of linen along the neckline marks the move away from heavy lace collars.

88 Thomas Chiffinch, c. 1656
S. Bourdon (attr.)

Note Men were also shown in informal dress, but as with their female counterparts there were always fashionable elements in their appearance.

Head The hair is brushed out from a central parting into a full, bushy style to just shoulder level.

Body The high collar of the doublet is unbuttoned but indicates the height which allowed a linen collar to sit so smoothly under the chin. A short row of buttons allows the doublet to fall away from the centre of the chest to reveal the shirt. Very full shirt sleeves were usual. The panes of the doublet sleeve are attached to a broad band loosely knotted at the inner arm.

89 Mrs Elizabeth Claypole, 1658
J. M. Wright

Note Daughter of Lord Protector Cromwell, Mrs Claypole is dressed in a manner befitting a *ci-devant* princess, in a breast-plate, and surrounded by allegorical symbols.

Head The position of the knot of hair can be seen at the back of the head with some of the curls pinned away from the face up to the knot.

Body A loosely held cloak reveals the edge of the smock and the full, layered ruffles around the sleeves. The skirt is held up, partly obscuring the central band of decoration but showing the braid at the hem and the lining beneath.

Accessories The jewellery is the traditional mixture of pearls and gemstone clasps.

90 Colonel the Honourable John Russell, 1659
J. M. Wright

Note The accoutrements of war and the commander's coloured sash do not detract from the nonchalant, billowing elegance of the dress.

Head The hair is longer, but still fairly full. A pencil-thin moustache is barely visible on an otherwise clean-shaven face.

Body The shallow collar is shorter at the front, raised above the ornate tassels. The buff jerkin has a natural waistline and its front lacing is matched by decorative lacing around the armholes. The wide doublet sleeves are tied in a bow on the inner arm, at a distance which allows the lower shirt sleeve edge to pouch over the wrist, with the wide, starched lace cuff standing away from the arm like a halo. The top of the breeches indicates that they are wide and loose-fitting.

91 Lady Jane Fisher, c. 1660
Unknown artist

Note An example of the mixture of formality and simplicity of dress which owes something to the much admired 'timeless' draperies.

Head The side hair is full, worn in ringlets of varying length and complemented by curls around the forehead and temples.

Body The low oval neckline of the stiff bodice is edged with a gauzy scarf. The armhole has dropped from the shoulder to the upper arm, and the full sleeve, taken in above the elbow to create a ruffle below, is loosely fitted, with the smock sleeve pouching out below it. The obliquely round centre front of the bodice, seen below the arm, flattens the front of the skirt, pushing all fullness to the sides and back of the waist. A gauze scarf is looped round the right shoulder.

92 Two ladies of the Lake family, c. 1660
Sir P. Lely

Note The informal pose and both artist's and sitters' attachment to soft draperies are exemplified in this portrait.

Head Both women wear softly cascading ringlets, with a looser hairdressing at the front which breaks the severe line of hair taken back from the forehead.

Body The bodice neckline is very wide, broken only by a glimpse of smock, and the lower inset of the sleeves emphasizes this horizontal line. The woman with the lute wears a smoothly fitting bodice over stays, but her companion is dressed in a looser, informal bodice held by clasps over the smock. Full sleeves and billowing smock sleeves are partly hidden by soft scarves.

93 James, Duke of York, c. 1661
Sir P. Lely

See colour plates, between pp. 96 and 97.

94 Charles II entering the City of London, 1661
D. Stoop

Note Although many of the men are wearing ceremonial uniforms, the group around the King are dressed in the height of fashion for the time.

Head The long, full, centrally parted hair may by now already be enhanced with pieces of false hair.

Body Shaped collars with ornate tassels are worn over short, loosely fitting jackets with open sleeves, caught above the wrist and edged with loops of ribbon. The wide 'petticoat' breeches are worn above the knee, braided or edged at waist and bottom edge with ribbons.

Accessories Deep falls of linen are a new, exuberant style of garter. High-heeled shoes with long narrow toes are tied with soft bows and the tall crowned hats are decorated with feathers or more ribbons.

95 James, Duke of York, 1661
S. Cooper

Note A closer view of the men's hairdressing and neckwear of the early Restoration period.

Head Men's hair is now longer and fuller than was fashionable earlier in the seventeenth century. It is coaxed here into soft waves and ringlets, arranged carefully to fall in symmetrical locks over the chest and back.

Body The linen collar, edged with lace is broad and deep but constructed to be shorter at the front and to curve under itself when tied. The full open sleeves of the jacket are of a brocaded silk edged with deep bands of braid.

**96 Lady Castlemaine, later Duchess of
Cleveland, 1664**
S. Cooper

Note The easy informality of everyday dress is
in contrast to the lavish fashions worn by women
at Court.

Head The ringlets framing the face escape
from beneath a carefully arranged hood which is
wide and deep enough not to crush the hairstyle.
The long sides of the hood are brought round
and tied beneath the chin, and a pin probably
secures it at the back of the head.

Body The smock is pulled casually over the
edge of the stiffened bodice and folded and
pinned to provide a simple collar. A soft scarf is
draped loosely round the arms.

97 Sir William Bruce, c. 1664
J. M. Wright

Note A Scottish gentleman architect dressed in
the informal Indian gown, a precursor of the
modern dressing gown.

Head In the early 1660s it is often hard to
differentiate between thick natural hair carefully
dressed to give bulk and the newly fashionable
periwig. Sir William's hair may be his own, with
the addition of some false pieces. A thin
moustache was an optional fashion, but one
favoured by the King.

Body Around the neck is knotted a long length
of linen, tied in a loose bow with the lace edges
displayed at the front. The striped robe is one of
the loose Indian gowns, of the type purchased by
Pepys at about this time. They were popular for
informal wear over a shirt and breeches.

98 9th Earl of Argyll and his countess, 1664 – 1665
Unknown artist

Note A fashionable couple whose interest in dress has transcended any urge to be informally draped in the classical manner.

Head The earl's hair is a wig with his natural hair brushed out over the forehead. The countess's ringlets are rising higher towards the temples and away from the face.

Body The lace of the earl's collar is different in design but compatible with the embroidery on the wide flaring cuffs. The jacket is short, partly unbuttoned, highly decorated, revealing the shirt and the beribboned top of the petticoat breeches. Lady Argyll is dressed in a tightly fitted, long-fronted bodice with full sleeves, and a matching skirt. Her smock has a gathered top, a formal edge above the bodice, complemented by crisp gathered ruffles attached to the sleeves.

99 Queen Catherine of Braganza, c. 1664
J. Huysmans (attr.)

Note A semi-formal state portrait of Charles II's queen which owes more to fashion than to artistic conventions.

Head The hair is full and higher at the sides of the head, presenting a structured width softened by tendrils of hair on the face.

Body The smock top is glimpsed over the decolletage of the stiffened bodice, with its long narrow front. The paned sleeves billow loosely over the full smock sleeves, but fit closely on the upper arms. The skirt is narrower, with no obvious bulk of material around the waist. A loose, gauzy scarf, shot with metal thread, possibly Indian in origin, is worn asymmetrically around the neckline.

Accessories The jewellery is the traditional mixture of pearls and gemstones.

12 Edward Sackville, 4th Earl of Dorset, 1613
W. Larkin

Note Even the most subdued colour scheme could be transformed into rich flamboyance by the addition of surface decoration and lavish accessories.

Head The full hairstyle, brushed away from the face, echoes the hair-dressing worn by women at this date (see 13).

Body The wide standing collar, supported on a pickadil, is of the finest Italian lace, so transparent that the doublet cuff can be glimpsed beneath the matching cuffs. A closely fitting doublet, open to display a few inches of linen shirt, is matched in silk, and in the scale of embroidery, by the high-heeled shoes. The heavy shoulder cape and wide breeches also reflect similar colour, material and decoration.

Accessories The flamboyantly lace-edged garters are *en suite* with the shoe rosettes, only the jewellery of narrow black cords is subdued and discreet. The ornately decorated hat on the table is a ceremonial accessory.

25 Unknown lady, 1618
M. Gheeraedts (the inscription is later, and inaccurate)

Note The narrower line of later Jacobean women's dress was matched by a diminution of decoration, and a stronger reliance on lustrous materials.

Head An aigrette adds height to the flatter, less formal hairstyle, and a shallow lace ruff isolates the head from the low decolletage of the bodice.

Body The deep oval neckline, edged with rosettes, recalls the formal style of bodice associated with Court dress (see 21), although the higher waistline distorts the balance of bodice and skirt. Contrasting fitted sleeves, and richly lined hanging over-sleeves focus attention on the upper part of the body and balance the elongated line of the skirt.

Accessories Discreet applied decoration and subtle textile motifs are enlivened by the deep lace cuffs, feather fan and rosette-trimmed shoes. The delicate jewellery is in harmony with the plain, everyday gloves on the chair.

47 Queen Henrietta Maria, 1633-1635
Unknown artist

Note The elegance of dress associated with female fashions at the Caroline Court owed more to simplicity of decoration and richness of colour than to ease of style.

Head The Queen's hair is teased into small curls which frame the sides of the face, and the knot at the back is surmounted by a delicate pearl tiara.

Body The low-cut bodice is edged by a deep collar which partly disguises the awkward set of the bulky sleeves, but the tension on the satin created by the high waistline is evident in the creases above the curved stomacher tab. The fullness in the skirt is drawn to the back of the waist and supported on hip pads. The applied pearl decoration adds interest and elongation of line to the essentially simple construction of bodice and skirt.

Accessories Pearl earrings and necklace complement the applied decoration on bodice and skirt. The coloured fan leaf is linked to the dress by the use of matching ribbons on the bosom and at the waistline.

76 3rd Viscount Fairfax of Emley and his wife, 1645-1648
G. Soest

Note The loose draperies which swag the dress of these two sitters do not disguise an interest in fashion seemingly unaffected by the exigencies of the Civil War.

Head Lord Fairfax's hair is of the intermediate length worn by the majority of young men in the mid-late 1640s. Lady Fairfax wears the loose, full side curls and smooth top hair which, growing in width, distorts the natural shape of the head.

Body His shallow collar tied with tasselled cords is at variance, in its practicality, with the full shirt sleeves which fall below the doublet cuffs. Her bodice has a dropped shoulder line which restrains the movements of the arms and upper body, but draws attention to the broad sweep of bosom and shoulders. The simplicity of the dress, with short sleeves and plain, untrimmed smock, is compensated for by the richly coloured satin and pretty jewelled clasps.

93 James, Duke of York, c.1661
Sir P. Lely

Note The military elements of the Duke's dress are diminished and masked by the exuberant use of material which characterized Restoration costume.

Head The combination of straggling hair over the forehead, and the long, thick, waving side locks suggest a judicious use of false hair to increase the natural bulk.

Body A long linen band is loosely knotted at the neck, its fullness complemented by billowing shirt sleeves framed by the silk of the doublet sleeves. A broad silk military sash masks much of the breast plate which is worn over a buff coat. Full satin breeches are edged with ribbon loops similar to those which trim the doublet sleeves, and the plain stockings are obscured by broad, tiered garters. Yet more ribbons are found as ties on the high-fronted shoes. The most overt military symbol is the military commander's baton.

120 Dame en habit de ville, 1678
J. le Pautre

Note A fashionably dressed young woman in outdoor clothes is attended by a page in a typical servant's livery.

Head A lace hood is arranged loosely over the upswept hairstyle, and an extra effect is created by the floating gauze scarf pinned over the hood.

Body The side view of the bodice displays the horizontal layers of collar, the shallow sleeve and the gathered tiers and ruffles of the smock rendered three-dimensional by the addition of ribbon loops. The trained skirt is looped back to reveal two contrasting petticoats, the lower one narrower and lacking a train. The page's dress has all the fashionable elements but in a stylized combination which does not allow for personal preference in details.

Accessories Elbow-length gloves and a bracelet muff provide the young woman with accessories which are practical and decorative.

141 Homme de qualité en habit garny de rubans, 1689
J. D. de St Jean

Note The exquisite grooming which French Court protocol demanded from courtiers is epitomized in this fashion plate.

Head The tightly curled wig is much higher above the forehead, carefully framing the face and falling back over the shoulders and away from the tiered cravat with its stiffened ribbon wings.

Body The body of the coat is fitted with the fullness of the skirts taken into side pleats. The pleated, pendant sleeves reveal a proportion of the rich brocade of the narrower waistcoat sleeves. Plain breeches, stockings and shoes do not draw attention away from the cascade of ribbons and the lace-edged sword hanger which decorate the upper half of the torso.

Accessories The hat is edged with feathers and more ribbons, and the gloves are worn to show the way the bullion fringe falls, either in a line with the glove, or over the wrist.

148 Marie Sophie Palatine, Reyne de Portugal, 1694
Unknown artist

Note An example of the type of fashion plate which incorporated pieces of appropriate material cut to fit within the outline drawing of a dress.

Head The increasing height of the fontange required an upswept hair-style to balance it; this example has long lace streamers or lappets.

Body The velvet mantua has elbow-length, loosely fitted sleeves with contrasting silk cuffs which match the bodice facings and skirt lining. The lace edge of the smock is displayed above the brocaded silk stomacher, and is complemented by deep, pendant lace sleeve ruffles. The upper petticoat is of a Chinese silk damask and the tiered effect is enhanced by the scalloped lower edge with its deep fringe, beneath which a striped brocade petticoat is worn.

Accessories Plain gloves and a fan are the only accessories. Patches on the face, depending on their placement, could convey unspoken messages or, more mundanely, disguise blemishes.

100 Sir John Harman, c. 1666
After Sir P. Lely

Note There were no naval uniforms in the seventeenth century, and this illustration shows the sitter wearing an early form of coat.

Head The hair appears to be Sir John's own, with some additional bulk added below the temples.

Body The loosely knotted linen cravat and the somewhat shapeless coat are reminiscent of Sir William Bruce (see 97), but the narrower lines of this coat, with cuffs which could be turned back, indicate that this is a version of the Persian vest (an early style of long coat) introduced to the English Court in 1666. In its early form it was rather experimental and various combinations of coat and waistcoat were tried, settling down into an accepted combination in the late 1670s.

101 Sir Norton Knatchbull, 1667
G. P. Harding after S. van Hoogstraaten

Note A lawyer in a modified, almost Quaker-like version of the new style of men's dress.

Head The natural hair is worn long.

Body Plain collars were worn by those unable to afford lace, or unwilling to waste money on such luxuries. A closely fitted waistcoat, with fuller skirts, buttoned to the waist is worn under a loose coat with shallow cuffs. The coat lining is revealed, and on the coat edge, on the upper-left-hand side of the chest, are a row of fastenings.

102 Unknown Couple, c. 1667
Unknown artist

Note In a pastoral setting, a fashionable young couple wear clothes which are adopted to suit her passive and his active pursuits.

Head The woman's hairstyle is very full at the sides of the head, with the ringlets suspended away from the face. Flat-brimmed straw hats protect the face from sunshine. The man wears a full wig under a broad beaver hat.

Body The woman's dress has a long, stiffened bodice, a soft scarf round the neck and shorter sleeves; the skirt is pushed back revealing a decorated petticoat. The man's coat is semi-fitted, buttoned to the waist, with deep cuffed full sleeves decorated with a knot of ribbons on the right shoulder.

Accessories Below the full breeches the riding boots still have wide, decorated tops.

103 Lord David Hay, c. 1667
D. Scougall

Note A young man dressed in the height of fashion.

Head Although still a beardless youth, Lord David wears a full, curling wig, from under which tendrils of his natural hair escape onto his forehead.

Body A deep, curving lace collar is worn with the straight unbuttoned tunic (coat) with short, deep cuffed sleeves which reveal the matching buttoned vest (waistcoat). The richly metallic brocade is woven with a vertical stripe which emphasizes the long, straight lines of this style. The looped ribbons on the sleeves and the billowing shirt sleeves alleviate the shapeless vertical line.

105 Jane Monins, Lady Knatchbull, c. 1669
J. M. Wright

Note A rare but visually accurate depiction of the informal nightgown.

Head Lady Knatchbull's hair is softer, less artificially ordered than was usual on formal occasions.

Body She is dressed in a low-necked, informal nightgown, with a closed bodice over boned stays. The fullness of the sleeves and easy, semi-fitted line of the skirt were understandably popular when formal dress required rigid, constricting fit. The smock sleeves are pushed above the elbows and held by jewelled bands which complement the brooches holding the gauzy scarf around the neckline.

104 Mary Beale, c. 1668
Self-portrait

Note A self-portrait in which the sitter, as artist, prefers the relaxed, informal draperies to the rigid lines of fashionable dress.

Head The hairstyle is full over the temples and above the forehead, reflecting the style of the fashionable world, but not attempting its pendant ringlets.

Body The loose, easily fitting dress with moderately full short sleeves, could be a deliberate artistic attempt to eliminate the stiffened bodice, or it may be a nightgown, a loose gown worn informally, offering greater comfort and ease of movement than the formal styles. The silk scarf is an accepted way of trimming the neckline, but its additional length transforms it here into a piece of drapery consistent with the pseudo-classical genre of portraiture.

106 Figures *à la Mode,* **c. 1670**
R. de Hoogh

Note One of a series of illustrations of the fashionable world by a Dutch engraver, possibly inspired by a visit to France.

Head The women's curls and ringlets emerge from the edges of the unfastened hood; the man's long curls are naturalistic enough to be his own hair.

Body The rigidity of the woman's bodice, with its long narrow front, and constricting short sleeves, is in contrast to the long, softly gathered skirt and petticoat. The man is dressed in the traditional style of long cape, short doublet and full, petticoat breeches. The ribbon decoration on the clothes is a reflection of the popularity of exuberant surface decoration. The figures in the background display varying silhouettes, all sharing a swaggering fullness.

108 Unknown woman, 1671
Unknown artist

Note This crudely painted but informative miniature records the tradition of sitters who wished to emulate the semi-formal appearance and manner of fashionable beauties.

Head The hairstyle lacks the upward movement and fullness at the sides and on the crown of the head which were popular in fashionable circles.

Body The shorter sleeves of the bodice and its overall narrow line, boned but worn directly over the smock rather than with stays, are a modest attempt at informality as is the discreet width of scarf, which imitates the fashionable accessory. The sleeves of the smock, caught in two places, demonstrate the tiered fashion which directed attention to this part of the dress.

107 William Legge, c. 1670
After J. Huysman

Note The dress of the soldier kept in step with fashion and provides small, but significant evidence of details for anyone attempting to reconstruct a broad view of men's fashions.

Head The full wig is exuberantly curled and fairly long.

Body The shirt collar is just visible over a billowing cravat which echoes the fullness of the shirt sleeves. The buff coat is similar in shape to the newly fashionable civilian coat, with open sleeves edged with ribbon loops. Below the military sash the ribbons are in keeping with the decoration usually found at the waist of breeches worn with an open tunic.

109 Thomas Sydserff, c. 1672
J. M. Wright

Note A Scottish bishop dressed in a comfortably simple version of the tunic and vest (see 103).

Head The wig is looser, more informally dressed than was fashionable in London.

Body Various styles of neckwear were worn in the 1670s, but the shorter, tiered lace cravat was increasingly popular from the early 1670s. Sir Thomas appears to be wearing a sleeveless tunic over his buttoned vest, which is made from the striped silk which appeared in this decade. The cuffs of the vest are not caught back, although the fold line is apparent. The waistband of the shirt sleeves is edged with a ribbon tie complementing the ribbon around the cravat.

110 The family of Sir Robert Vyner, 1673
J. M. Wright

Note This group illustrates the importance of children in late-seventeenth-century portraits, as their dress reflects current fashions often more accurately than that of their elders.

Head Lady Vyner's hair is dressed in a mass of curls and ringlets and Sir Robert's wig is longer but equally full at the sides of the head.

Body Both adults wear loose robes; hers is held by one clasp, partly revealing the stiffened bodice and striped brocaded silk of her skirt; his is a robe, tied with a sash, worn over a linen shirt with lace collar and cuffs. The girl's dress has the formal fashionable elements of wide neckline, flat, stiff bodice and short sleeves over full, tiered smock sleeves. The lace is delicate and complementary to the pale silk. The boy wears a loose-fitting vest with short, ribbon-bedecked sleeves, with matching ribbons at the waist.

111 *Habit de ville,* **1673**
J. D. de St. Jean

Note The French fashion plates which appeared in the 1670s have no English equivalent, but are crucial sources of information for fashionable dress in both countries.

Head The formal curls, assisted by false hair, stand away from the face, and their width is exaggerated by the frilled band and veil pinned to the back of the head.

Body A broad lace collar masks the decolletage of the rigid bodice and much of the short sleeve. The tiered effect of the sleeves is constructed from lace ruffles, ruched smock sleeves and ribbon bows. The skirt is looped back to display the rich brocade petticoat.

Accessories Elbow-length gloves, a painted fan and high-heeled shoes were essential accessories at this time.

112 2nd Viscount Brouncker, c. 1673
After Sir Peter Lely?

Note Although apparently timeless, and classically severe in its draperies, the sitter's usual dress is not wholly disguised.

Head A full wig and narrow moustache were affected by many courtiers in emulation of the King.

Body A simple linen and lace cravat is worn with a long coat, with the short sleeves and loosely turned back cuffs of the early 1670s. The button-holes of the coat, reaching to the hem, can be seen, as can the full breeches with their knots of ribbons at the knee. The raised right hand reveals the narrow wrist band of the shirt sleeve to which the deep ruffled cuff is attached.

113 Duke and Duchess of Lauderdale, c. 1674
Sir P. Lely

Note Contrasting styles of dress: the man proudly formal, wearing Garter insignia, the woman in the informal dress of her own apartments.

Head The duke is wearing a formal wig, still fairly flat on the crown, but now full at the sides. The duchess's hair is loosely dressed, but is fairly wide.

Body He is wearing a coat, only partly buttoned under the deep, lace-edged collar, with short sleeves buttoned back in a cuff, and a knot of ribbons on the right shoulder. His breeches are decorated with looped ribbons at waist and knee. The duchess is informally dressed in a nightgown, buttoned low over the smock. The latter has the fashionable short, tiered sleeves.

Accessories A light gauze scarf is her only accessory.

114 Mary of Modena, Duchess of York, c. 1674
Sir P. Lely

Note An informal portrait, but not wholly lacking the rigidity of fashionable dress.

Head The hair has been carefully curled but then allowed to spring loosely away from the head in calculated informality.

Body The long-fronted bodice is much stiffer than is usual when the smock is revealed between the front clasps. The soft, full sleeves with the panes held together with jewelled clasps are an artistic convention, which might have been worn informally, but owe little to either high fashion or nightgown styles.

Accessories The gauze scarf and simple jewellery were accepted accessories in the post-Restoration period.

115 The Baths at Bath, 1675
T. Johnson

Note Drinking the waters or bathing at spas was popular with men and women of all social classes in the seventeenth century.

Head The majority of the men wear wide-brimmed hats over their hair, which ranges from the natural, straggling variety to the full, long wigs. All of the women wear hoods.

Body The rather shapeless, inelegant line of men's coats is well illustrated by the rows of figures watching the bathing. Breeches vary between the wide tubular style edged with ribbon loops and the closer-fitting style with a knee-band. The short-sleeved, fitted bodices and open skirts of the women's dress are all taken back to display the petticoats, and provide a backview of fashions similar to 111.

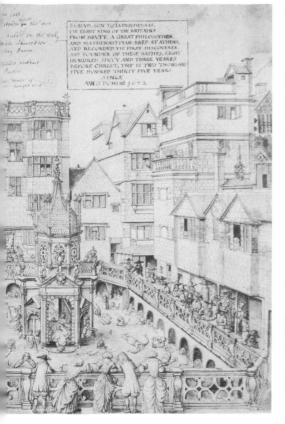

116 1st Earl of Bath, 1676
J. M. Wright

Note The sitter was Keeper of the Wardrobe to Charles II and an influential and fashionable courtier.

Head The long, smooth wig and narrow moustache are insignificant foils to the grandeur of the earl's dress.

Body The tiered cravat is composed of layers of fine linen overlaid with lace. His richly embroidered coat, with its deeply cuffed sleeves, is so ornately decorated that the loose, inelegant line of cut is barely noticeable. No waistcoat distracts attention from the lace-edged shirt front, or from the wide petticoat breeches with their ribbon points at the waist. Matching ribbons decorate the cuffs and form a shoulder knot.

Accessories The broad embroidered sash, *en suite* with the coat, acts as a sword hanger, and the earl's key of office is suspended from the rosette at his waist.

117 *Habit de ville,* 1676
N. Bonnart

Note The formality of fashionable female dress owed more to the style of
bodice than to other, less restricting elements.

Head A light scarf is pinned casually to the back of the tightly curled hair.

Body The vertical line of the bodice is emphasized by wide bands of braid
which stress its angular narrowness. The smock sleeves are decorated with
additional ruffles and ribbons which create a softer silhouette. The long,
trained skirt was, by now, invariably looped back into a low bustle,
revealing the petticoats, in this instance, two contrasting ones.

Accessories The gloves have a shallow frill, complementing the sleeves'
ruffles, whilst the shoes reflect the narrow, attenuated shape of the bodice,
but are softened by ribbon ties.

118 Charles II receiving a pineapple from Rose the gardener, c. 1676
After N. Danckerts

Note The two main characters wear the new style of coat, and only the details of their dress distinguish King from gardener.

Head Both men wear full wigs, but only the King wears a hat: wide brimmed, but with a shallow crown.

Body Their neckwear, bands of fabric, not quite cravats, are of linen for the gardener, lace for the King; and the latter has matching sleeve ruffles. Their plain coats, loosely fitting with low set buttoned pockets, have contrasting cuffs decorated with ribbons, and each man has a knot of ribbons on the right shoulder. The King's full breeches are fairly short, revealing a good deal of leg covered with plain stockings.

Accessories The King wears narrow-fronted shoes with a deep flap or tongue above the fastening and buckle.

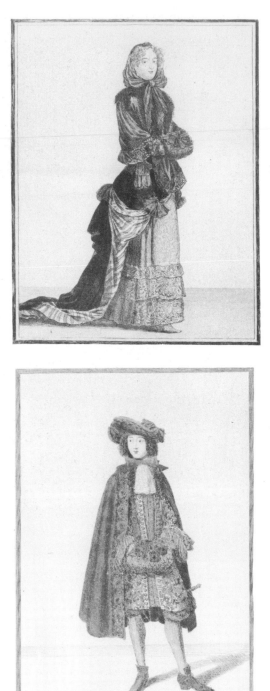

119 *La dame de grand air*, **1677**
N. Bonnart

Note A fashionable woman dressed warmly for winter weather.

Head A hood is tied under the chin, with curls brought forward over the temples.

Body A fur tippet, matching the muff, is worn over a shoulder cape edged with lace. The bustle effect of the skirt is emphasized by an arrangement of ribbons which look too permanent for the skirt to be worn in any other manner. The contrasting materials of the skirt and its dramatic lining, and the patterned petticoat edged with deep lace flounces, draw attention to the lower area of the body.

Accessories Leather gloves are worn in addition to the fur muff.

120 *Dame en habit de ville*, **1678**
J. le Pautre

See colour plates, between pp. 96 and 97.

121 *Homme de qualité en habit d'hiver*, **1678**
J. D. de St. Jean 1678

Note Fashion plates provide invaluable information regarding seasonal variations in dress.

Head The young man's wig is full at the sides of the head, narrows at the neck and descends in two long ringlets onto his chest. The shape of his hat foreshadows the later tricorne as the brim is shaped and begins to turn up at front and back.

Body The lace band is enlivened by a wide bow partly masking the collar of the long cape. The coat is worn open to reveal the fully buttoned, contrasting long-sleeved waistcoat, the cuffs of which are taken back over the coat cuffs. The breeches are fairly narrow, with the fullness above the knee.

Accessories Fringed gloves are worn for extra warmth with the large fur muff.

122 *Dame en deshabille de ville,* **1678**
J. le Pautre

Note Fashionable and acceptable informal
dress.

Head Full curls are pushed over the forehead,
and a shallow-frilled cap is worn under the
hood.

Body A lace-edged shoulder cape is pulled
round the bodice, of a length to provide warmth
but without masking the line of the skirt. The
evolution of a contrived bustle arrangement is
now almost complete, with the skirt looped up
and back and held so that the pattern of the skirt
material and its lining are seen to advantage.
The petticoat is *en suite* with the skirt, but with a
deep band of lace attached at the hem.

123 Sir Leoline Jenkins, 1679
H. Tuer

Note A diplomat and statesman of mature years, dressed sombrely but in
keeping with fashionable taste.

Head Sir Leoline's curling wig is shorter, falling to the shoulder.

Body His linen and lace collar is of the traditional full shaped variety. The
large, sinuous floral motifs of the lace are well recorded by the painter on
both collar and cuffs. The coat is plain and narrow, with deep, turned-back
cuffs, and a large knot of ribbons on the right shoulder. Full shirt sleeves
remained an important feature of men's dress until the coat sleeves
lengthened in the next decade.

124 Charles II and Queen Catherine, 1682
Engraved frontispiece from Ogilby's and
Morgan's *Map of London*

Note A Court private presentation in which all
of the figures wear semi-formal dress.

Head All the men, with the exception of Ogilby
(kneeling), wear curled wigs, but only the King
wears a hat. The universal fashion of wearing
hats indoors disappeared around c. 1680. The
broad, tightly curled hairstyles of the ladies echo
the shape, if not the length of the male styles.

Body Softly gathered cravats, full shirts with
ruffled cuffs, and full breeches are worn with the
ubiquitous loose coats with their assemblage of
buttons. Coat sleeves are longer, but retain wide
cuffs. Stiff, long-fronted bodices are worn with
looped up, trained skirts over patterned
petticoats.

Accessories All the women wear elbow-length
gloves and pearl jewellery. Their narrow-toed
shoes are similar in style to those of the men.

125 Duchess of Portsmouth, 1682
P. Mignard

Note An elegantly informal Court beauty, one of Louis XIV's 'subsidies' to Charles II, whose mistress she became.

Head The arrangement of the duchess's hair is carefully calculated: tight curls, softened by a coiled ringlet and a knot of hair entwined with pearls.

Body The smock is edged at the neck and sleeve edges by delicately wrought lace, almost certainly French in origin. The richly brocaded formal silk of the dress is at variance with the semi-informal style: lightly boned but lacking the rigidity of fashionable formal dress. The contrasting sleeves are in keeping with the pseudo-classical/pastoral genre.

Accessories The jewellery is discreet but impressive in its mixture of pearls and gemstones.

Essex Buildings, *The Temple*, *A Show Booth*, *Nine pins Playing*, *A Chariot with 3 Wheels moved by screws*, *The Booth with A Phenix on it and inspired for long of the foundation stand*, *The Bull Baiting*, *Hunting a Fox*, *Roasting the Ox*, *Sliding holes*, *One sliding in A hutch Moved by a stick*, *Printing Booth*, *Coals Carried on Sledges*, *The boat drawn with a Horse*, *Boyes Sliding*, *A Whirling Sledg*, *playing at Vigeor holes*, *Temple*, *Street*, *The Drum Boat*, *A Youth Walking on Stilts*, *Foot-ball Playing*, *Men throwing at Cock*

126 An English couple, 1683
Engraving from *Description de l'Univers . . .*

Note Distinctions in dress between European countries existed throughout the seventeenth century, although France provided much inspiration for English fashions.

Head The flamboyantly curling wig of the man is balanced by a broad-brimmed beaver hat. The woman's hair is brought forward over the forehead beneath the light scarf.

Body The combination of cravat and flat bow was popular for men in the 1680s, masking the flat, insignificant coat neckline. Vertical or low-level horizontal slits were equally acceptable pocket openings. Full breeches, a sword hanger and a decorative sash enliven the plain coat. The woman's dress is typical of the style of the early 1680s (see 124) with the skirt held up to prevent staining.

Accessories Both wear plain gloves, the woman's with a frilled edge. The walking stick and fan were fashionable optional accessories.

127 Frost Fair on the Thames, 1684
Unknown artist

Note Crude sketches, like cartoons, often capture the essentials of personal appearance, although they lack detail.

Head In this large group of mixed social background, all the men wear or hold shallow-brimmed hats. Some wear wigs, others have shorter natural hair. The women all wear hoods.

Body Small cravats are worn by all the men with their semi-fitted coats, some of which have horizontal pocket flaps. The coats are worn closed against the cold above moderately full breeches. The women wear short capes or shawls above their skirts, and, in essentials, they have a bulkier, less balanced silhouette than the men.

117

128 *Dame en escharpe,*
1685
N. Bonnart

Note This
exaggerated French
fashion was not copied
in England, although
certain elements of the
dress were more
widely popular.

Head The hair is
smoother, taken back
from the forehead and
decorated with
stiffened bows, a large
gauze scarf framing
the head and
shoulders.

Body A lace cape
with long front panels
masks the bodice. The
trained skirt is looped
up in complex folds,
held with bows, and
would have needed a
frame or substantial
pad to achieve this
height. The top
petticoat is
complementary, in its
looped folds, to the
skirt, but the under-
petticoat trails on the
ground.

Accessories Masks
were convenient
disguises as well as,
supposedly, protecting
the complexion.

129 Lady of quality, 1685 – 1686
Unknown artist

Note One of the few English fashion plates of the late seventeenth century, but obviously much influenced by its French counterparts.

Head The hair is taken back from the face in soft waves, surmounted by ribbons and lightly held within a loosely knotted scarf.

Body The dress, perhaps glimpsed earlier (128) is the new style of gown or mantua. This developed from the loose-fitting informal gown. The bodice and skirt are attached at the normal waistline, with the excess bodice material pleated on each front to fit over the stays beneath. A contrasting stomacher, or decorated stays panel, was pinned to the bodice and held by a narrow belt. The overskirt has formalized into neat folds around the hips.

Accessories One gloved hand draws attention to the watch suspended from the waist.

Homme de qualité en habit d'esv

130 *Homme de qualité en habit d'espée*, **c. 1685**
Unknown artist

Note The more structured line of men's coats is a feature of the mid/late 1680s, when loose-fullness was gradually giving way to a defined silhouette.

Head Short curly hair or short wigs seem to have been a passing, little-copied fashion.

Body The carefully arranged cravat and upturned ribbons suit the closer-fitting line of the coat, the vertical emphasis reinforced by narrower sleeves and breeches. The residual swagger, baroque decoration, knot of shoulder ribbons, loose cuffs, diagonal sword hanger and billowing shirt sleeves are retained.

Accessories The narrower, upward-curling brim of the hat is closer to a tricorne, and the long-fronted leather shoes have coloured heels in the French manner.

119

131 Coronation Procession of James II, 1686
Engraving from Sandford's *History of the Coronation of James II*

Note A scene of state ceremonial in which, apart from the figures in
traditional robes, the grandest male fashions are worn.

Head The line of men in the foreground all wear shallow brimmed hats,
lavishly trimmed with feathers, over their full wigs.

Body The unfitted line of their coats, falling from the shoulders like
smocks, is broken only by open side seams and vertical lines of braid and
embroidery. Horizontal pockets are higher, but lack flaps. The sleeves
have deep cuffs, above ruffled shirt sleeves. Only the man to the far left has
adopted the more fitted, shorter coat with minimal side pleats and angled
cuffs.

Accessories All the men wear high-fronted shoes held by buckles.

132 The Chariot of the Virgin Queen, Lord Mayor's Pageant, 1686
Unknown artist

Note A festive, outdoor event, affording a lively but unusual London street scene.

Head A sea of men's hats with up-turned brims, worn over wigs and shorter natural hair, is leavened by female hoods over upswept hair, and one high-crowned woman's hat (right, centre front).

Body The change in men's coat design is carefully recorded; the upper body more fitted, the skirt width absorbed into full pleats at sides and back. Pockets vary between vertical and horizontal slits, with some horizontal flaps in evidence. Stockings are rolled over the knees of the closer fitting breeches. The women wear short-sleeved mantuas, with the skirts swagged back over the hips to display one or more petticoats.

133 *Femme de qualité en habit d'esté,* **1687**
N. Arnoult

Note The easy, but elegant line of the mantua quickly established it as the most important style for women.

Head Head-dresses were increasingly important in the late 1680s; composed of ribbons, tiers of lace frills and streamers, this style was called a cornet.

Body The mantua has a stomacher masked by ribbon bows: echelles. The trained skirt is looped round the hips and, held by ties or pins, falls in a cascade of folds from the back of the waist. The petticoat has a decorated open pocket slit, beneath which a separate pocket, tied round the waist, might hold a handkerchief. Striped materials remained popular often arranged in vertical and horizontal combinations.

Accessories Elbow-length gloves and pretty fans were essential accessories.

134 *Homme de qualité,* **1687**
J. D. de St. Jean

Note This young exquisite embodies the decorative flamboyance which could be superimposed on the fairly severe lines of men's dress.

Head The very full wig is probably powdered; its width allied to fashionable impulse dictates the rakish angle of the ornately trimmed hat.

Body A semi-fitted, long-sleeved waistcoat is worn with the coat; both garments are lavishly decorated with bands of applied metal lace and bullion fringe. Broad, pendant coat cuffs acted as a frame for waistcoat sleeves or, in other circumstances, the billow of shirt sleeves and ruffles. Moderately full breeches are worn to the knee.

Accessories The waterfall effect of the cravat over the knot of ribbons is echoed by the fringed gloves, with the weighted bullion fringe falling gracefully over the hand.

123

135 Frances Stuart, Duchess of Richmond and Lennox, 1687
W. Wissing and J. van der Vaart

Note 'La Belle Stuart', a famous beauty of Charles II's reign, is depicted in informal dress.

Head The backswept hair with tendrils around the face was also worn with more formal styles of dress (see 132), but the loose undressed hair falling over the shoulder is in character with the informality of dress and pose.

Body The duchess is dressed in a loose gown over a low-necked smock, and it is possible to deduce how, in the hands of a skilful sempstress, this type of garment had evolved into a mantua: opened at the front, the bodice pleated to fit over stays and stomacher, with the fullness of the skirt looped up around the hips. The robe and coronet probably refer to the duchess's presence at James II's coronation in 1686.

136 *Dame de qualité à l'eglise*, 1688
G. Jollain

Note When fashionable men and women attended church they wore their finest clothes and considered the occasion a social event.

Head Tight curls are crowned by a tiered lace cap over which two hoods, an inner, lightweight striped one, and an outer contrasting plain, are knotted.

Body The mantua bodice is masked by a lace shoulder cape and fur tippet, and a lace handkerchief is suspended from the waist. The page is a miniature, less flamboyantly dressed version of the young exquisite (134). Although to modern eyes such rich dress seems at odds with the idea of service, the page would have been recognized immediately by his contemporaries, identified by the livery colours of his master or mistress.

tot Calais en reyst na de koning van vrankryk tot S.

137 Arrival of Queen Mary of Modena in Calais (detail), 1688
Unknown artist

Note The easy, sketchy depiction of this scene captures the essence of late 1680s fashions in movement.

Head The Queen's male attendants have the short hair and skull caps of professional men: physicians, clerks, priests. The two Frenchmen are wearing wigs (the flatness of the back hair, around which the curls are arranged, is noticeable). The Queen and her ladies have upswept curls with low knots at the back of the hair, or high head-dresses.

Body The male refugees are bundled up in travelling capes, in contrast to the Frenchmen who wear the decorated coats and the swords of gentlemen courtiers. A maid of honour carries the Queen's train but the other ladies have to hold or pin up their skirts to assist movement.

138 The Squire of Alsatia, 1688
M. Laroon II

Note The *Cries of London*, from which this engraving is taken, are the longest series of English late-seventeenth-century engraved figures which concentrate on variations in dress.

Head The asymmetrical style of wig had appeared in France (see 134) and was copied in England. The squire's hat concentrates attention on the curved brim, braid-edged and feather-trimmed; no crown is visible.

Body The plainness of the coat and waistcoat are alleviated by the still popular rows of buttons: on the waistcoat, coat front, cuffs and pockets.

Accessories The lace and ribbon cravat, bullion-fringed gloves, walking stick and sword are the discreet but distinctive accessories of a gentleman.

50

139 Old Satten, Old Taffety or Velvet, 1688
M. Laroon II

Note There was an important secondhand
market in materials in the seventeenth century,
reflecting the high cost of the luxurious imported
silk textiles.

Head The street seller wears the traditional
conical crowned, wide-brimmed hat of the lower
classes, over her plain hood.

Body Her dress is a modest version of the
mantua. The pleating of the material to fit the
torso and to sit smoothly over the shoulders, and
the set of the short sleeves, are easier to see than
in French fashion plates. Her skirt is floor-length
and does not require careful arrangement of
folds, but hangs free, only a little longer than the
petticoat. The linen apron echoes the crisp
simplicity of the modestly ruffled smock sleeves.

Accessories The shoes are plain, not
exaggeratedly long-fronted, but tied with
ribbons, perhaps from the seller's own stock.

140 Old Cloaks, Suits or Coats, 1688
M. Laroon II

Note The trade in secondhand clothes operated
at all levels, from the imperceptibly worn clothes
of the fashionably rich through to the worn
oddments of the poor.

Head The clothes-seller wears his own hair
under the assortment of old-fashioned wide-
brimmed hats divested of their decoration.

Body A scrap of linen is tied at his throat as a
semblance of a cravat. A skimpy cape is worn
over a bedraggled coat: the loose, long-sleeved
variety with fewer and larger buttons, which was
worn by working men. The plain breeches and
unmatched shoes are derived from even more
unsaleable stock than the oddments for sale that
are held in the seller's hand.

Accessories Only the two swords suggest that
gentlemen, or those with pretensions to gentility,
were likely to be amongst his customers.

141 *Homme de qualité en habit garny de rubans,*
1689
J. D. de St. Jean

See colour plates, between pp. 96 and 97.

142 *Femme de qualité allant incognito par la ville,*
1689
J. D. de St. Jean

Note Disguise, usually in the form of a mask,
was adopted by fashionable women when they
wished for anonymity; it might imply a secret
errand or meeting.

Head Tiered caps, called fontanges, supposedly
named after a mistress of Louis XIV, increased
in height at the end of the 1680s, producing a
distorted shape to the head when both cap and
hair were covered by a hood.

Body The mantua sleeves were longer and
looser, and the fit of the bodice was improving,
although in this illustration it is partly obscured
by a lace cape. The manner in which the skirt is
looped up suggests, rather unusually, a closed
front to the skirt, but the rich petticoat was
evidently chosen to be displayed rather than
concealed.

Accessories A tiny muff is pushed back over
the wrist of one gloved hand, and a black, paper
mask is held against the face.

143 Robert Boyle, 1689 – 1690
After J. Kerseboom

Note The comparative ease and comfort of men's coats did not diminish the appeal of the loose robe for informal dress.

Head Boyle's wig is long and luxuriantly curled; its length is balanced by a raised, double row of curls springing up from the central parting above the forehead.

Body The plain cravat, tied like a scarf, has narrow silk strips woven into the linen, and silk fringe trimming. The informal silk robe is worn over shirt and breeches. It was a perennially popular garment for gentlemen in the privacy of their home. A quick transformation could be achieved by discarding the robe and replacing it with a waistcoat and coat.

144 Church of St Mary Overy, Southwark (detail), 1689 – 1690
Unknown artist

Note Groups of people, seen in conjunction with a building, often contain a cross section of the population, and a context is provided for their dress.

Head Both women in the foreground wear fontanges, but of differing heights.

Body The silhouettes of the men (with the exception of the beggar) demonstrate the importance of personal taste in the progress of new styles of dress. The man in the centre foreground wears the loose-fitting coat of the mid-1680s whilst the men in the background have adopted the closer-fitting coats, with distinctive side pleats which had appeared subsequently. The mantua skirts of the two women in the foreground are looped up and back, and one has the additional warmth of a shoulder cape over her bodice. The two young girls (left foreground) wear the uniforms of charity schools.

130

145 The Holbein Gate, Whitehall Palace, 1690 – 1692
Unknown artist

Note Architectural draughtsmen usually deliniate the figures within their compositions sketchily, but manage to convey the essence of the prevailing fashions.

Head The women wear double-tiered forward-tilting fontages, with their hoods masking the small cap at the back of the head to which the wired lace frills were attached.

Body The men's coats are closely fitting with the fullness of the skirts taken into pleats at the sides and back. Their deep-cuffed sleeves are longer, allowing only the shirt-sleeve ruffles to be seen. The bulkiness around their knees is caused by the rolling of the stocking tops over the breeches, like a cuff. Both women wear capes and their skirts are pinned up high at the back of the waist to prevent the material trailing on the ground. They wear short aprons – decorative accessories made of lace, embroidered silk, gauze or linen – over their petticoats.

147 *Homme de qualité en habit garny d'agrémens,*
1693
J. D. de St. Jean

Note A studied informality characterizes the
dress of this young nobleman.

Head A moderate-sized hat is enlarged by deep
plumes decorating the curving brim. The wig is
worn casually pushed back over the shoulders.

Body An insouciant air is reinforced by the
expanse of linen shirt pouching over the top of
the breeches. A long linen cravat is worn in the
Steinkerk fashion: loosely twisted with its ends
pushed through a buttonhole of the coat. No
waistcoat is worn under the coat, and the latter is
decorated with a new arrangement of buttons.
They continue to run from neck to hem but are
grouped in threes on metal lace. Loose-fitting
breeches are balanced at the knees with rolled
stocking tops pushed above the garters.

Accessories Lace-edged gloves and high-
heeled shoes are fairly plain accessories,
although of distinctive cut.

146 *Dame de la plus haute qualité,* **1693**
J. D. de St. Jean

Note A young noblewoman dressed in the richest fashions of the early
1690s.

Head Above upswept hair the lace fontange has four tiers, decreasing in
width. Lace streamers or lappets fall from the sides of the cap around the
face to the middle of the back.

Body The silk mantua has loosely fitting elbow-length sleeves and a
stomacher decorated with echelles. The skirt is looped up and folded to
display the contrasting lining and the border embroidery. The striped,
brocaded silk petticoat is further enriched with applied bands of metal
fringe.

Accessories In addition to the usual pearl necklace and earrings, a locket
or miniature is tied onto the left wrist.

148 Marie Sophie Palatine, Reyne de Portugal, 1694
Unknown artist

See colour plates, between pp. 96 and 97.

149 1st Earl of Halifax, 1693 – 1694
Sir G. Kneller

Note Another version of informal dress draws on a simplified version of a real garment and marries it to swaggering, semi-classical draperies.

Head Lord Halifax's wig has the pronounced height above the forehead which was fashionable in the 1690s.

Body His plain linen cravat is arranged in the Steinkerk fashion (see 147) which reflects an attitude of studied informality. The close-fitting garment is cut like, and has all the features of, a waistcoat, but the decorative clasps are atypical, giving a familiar garment an unexpected, conservative grandeur.

Accessories A sword belt and hanger are worn round the waist, in the usual manner, under the coat, but over the waistcoat. A deep swag of silk drapery enhances the effect of supposed timelessness.

150 *Homme de qualité en habit de Teckeli,* **1694**
J. D. de St. Jean

Note The warfare in which France engaged at the end of the seventeenth century influenced men's dress: a military aspect overlaid the casual elegance.

Head The hat brim is curled close to the crown at the left side, improving the vision of the wearer, and the wig is less luxuriant, its ends twisted and knotted to shorten the impractical length.

Body A variant of the Steinkerk cravat is worn pushed under the striped waistcoat. The full-skirted coat has broad contrasting facings decorated with frogging (a style which continued to be associated with soldiers long after it passed out of general fashion).

Accessories Only the large fur muff, suspended from the waist on a belt, and the snuff box suggest a gentleman playing at being a soldier rather than the genuine article.

151 *Femme de qualité en deshabillé d'hyver,* **1694**
J. D. de St. Jean

Note Seasonal variations in dress revolved around the type and weight of silk, and fur accessories in winter-time; wool was not much worn by fashionable women.

Head The tiered fontange is surmounted by two small silk horns, and the hair is swept up into two oblique horns.

Body The mantua sleeves are fairly full and sleeve ruffles fall in graduated folds from below the cuffs. The skirt is pinned back over a pad or cage which emphasizes the bustle effect, and a long train trails behind. The brocaded silk petticoat is trimmed with applied fringe set in straight and scalloped horizontal bands.

Accessories Elbow-length gloves and a fan are joined by the winter accessories of a fur tippet and a small muff decorated with a silk bow.

**152 The Mercers' Chapel, Mercers Hall
(detail), c. 1695**
Unknown artist

Note Fashionable dress is placed here within
the context of an architecturally elegant London
street.

Head The two men in the foreground, although
sketchily drawn, have the two horn-like pyramids
of hair above the temples which were a fashionable feature of 1690s wigs. The woman's hair is
contained in a cap to which the fontange
decoration of tiered frills is attached.

Body The men's coats are well cut, fitting
closely to the upper torso, with swaggering skirts,
enlarged by full side pleats, and wrist-length
sleeves broadened by deep cuffs. The back of
the woman's bodice is close-fitting above the
looped bustle arrangement of the long skirt.

Accessories Both carry the newer style of hat: a
tricorne, which gradually replaced the earlier
styles of wide, curving-brimmed beavers.

154 Prince James Stuart (the 'Old Pretender') with his sister, 1695
N. de Largillière

Note Children were exquisitely dressed as miniature adults, but their portraits were less susceptible to informal, classical or drapery styles of painting.

Head The prince wears his own hair, shorter than a fashionable wig, but brushed up into peaks above the temples. The construction of his sister's fontange, with its graduated tiers of lace attached to a cap, is clearly visible.

Body The lace and ribbon cravat was accepted formal wear; the studied elegance of the brocaded waistcoat with cuffs turned over the coat cuffs, the stiff-skirted coat, buttoned just enough to display its fine cut, the leather shoes with contrasting tongue lining, the modified tricorne and the Garter orders and sword reflect the stylish rigidity of French Court circles. The princess's dress is a child's version (complete with leading strings) of the stiff-bodied gown which French royal ladies wore on great occasions in preference to a mantua.

153 *Habit de cavalier,* **1695**
J. Mariette

Note Another version of the semi-martial fashions associated with professional soldiers, and briefly with the fashionable world.

Head The new style of tricorne hat evolved from the shallow, curving-brimmed, low-crowned hats which had been easing towards a change in shape for some time. The wig is pushed back from the face over the back shoulders, a more practical arrangement for a soldier.

Body The coat has unusually full sleeves, as wide as the deep cuffs. The facings on the body of the coat are displayed, in the manner of revers, but from waist to hem the coat is fastened by buttons submerged within braided and tasselled frogging.

Accessories A large muff is worn almost as a decoration, suspended from the waist by a carefully tied ribbon sash.

137

156 6th Earl of Dorset, 1697
Sir G. Kneller

Note Men's dress had evolved into a stylish, easy elegance by the end of the seventeenth century despite the pomposity of their wigs.

Head The fullness of the wig above the forehead is no longer discernably in two sections but massed together, with the bulky length pushed back over the shoulders.

Body Lord Dorset's cravat is twisted around the throat and worn in a modified Steinkerk diagonal swathe below the velvet coat. The line of the coat neck is seen curving gently into the front edge. The braided fastenings and large buttons, grouped rather than in a long row, reflect the influence of French semi-military fashions (see 150, 153).

Accessories Lord Dorset holds his wand of office as Lord Chamberlain in his left hand.

155 John Dryden, 1696 – 1697
J. Maubert

Note A rare full-length portrait of a man in formal dress.

Head The long wig appears somewhat disordered, as if in need of the ministrations of its maker; the pyramids of hair above the temples are disarranged and lop-sided.

Body A fringed linen cravat is worn with a plain shirt with unadorned cuffs. The comfortable bulk of the satin robe, its wide sleeves, easy wrapover front and warm, ankle length are clearly displayed.

Accessories Dryden wears mules on his feet: low-heeled for ease of movement, but bullion-fringed to indicate taste and expense. These indoor slippers were popular, following the prevailing shape of shoe fronts but more comfortable to wear.

157 Studies of head-dresses, published 1703, drawn 1698 – 1701
B. Picart

Note Variations in a style of dress are illustrated by this group of five different head-dresses.

Head The five hairstyles are all subtly different: upswept smooth rolls of hair, upswept horns above the temples, curls teased onto the forehead, short ringlets and plain knots covered by caps. All of the fontanges are attached to gathered caps, one with loose streamers (top right), one with the streamers pinned up (bottom left). The tiered structures all curve forward but vary in their angle, height and width. The material is pleated and wired into its tiered designs.

Body The two top drawings show the folded edge of the mantua, pinned to a stomacher with the smock frills framing the neckline, the lower left drawing is of a *robe de chambre* with ruched trimming.

158 Choir of St Paul's Cathedral (detail), 1698 – 1700
Unknown artist

Note By the end of the century men's and women's dress had evolved into
the elegant but easy styles which were modified, refined but not dramatically
changed until the late eighteenth century.

Head All of the men wear the full broad wigs of the turn of the century,
with the considerable length pushed back over their shoulders. The
women's fontanges are diminishing in height (see 157).

Body The men's coats have the wider sleeves and proportionately
shallower cuffs from which only the sleeve ruffles emerge. The stiffly
pleated coat skirts were interlined to achieve this rigid line. All of the
pockets are horizontal, with flaps, and the tricorne hat is proving an easier
accessory; it can be pushed comfortably under one arm (foreground,
second left). The women's mantuas have fuller sleeves and their petticoats
are widening and developing a tiered, frilled silhouette.

Select Bibliography

Adburgham, A., *Women in Print*, Allen & Unwin, 1972
——, *Shopping in Style*, Thames & Hudson, 1979

Archibald, E.H.H., *Portraits at The National Maritime Museum 1570 – 1748*, HMSO, 1954

Arnold, J., *Patterns of Fashion I: 1660 – 1860*, Macmillan, 1972
——, *Perukes and Periwigs*, HMSO, 1970

Baines, B., *Fashion Revivals*, Batsford, 1981

Belknap Jnr, W.P., *American Colonial Painting, Materials for a History*, Belknap Press of University of Harvard Press, 1959

British Museum Department of Prints and Drawings, *Catalogue of Engraved British Portraits vols 1 – 6*, Trustees of the British Museum, 1908 – 1925

Byrde, P., *The Male Image*, Batsford, 1979

Corbett, M. & Norton, M., *Engraving in England* vol. *III: Charles I*, Cambridge University Press, 1964

Cumming, V., The Trousseau of Princess Elizabeth Stuart, *Collectanea Londiniensis*, Museum of London, 1978

Cunnington, C.W. & P., *Handbook of English Costume in the Seventeenth Century*, Faber & Faber, 1972

Cunnington, P. & Lucas, C., *Costume for Births, Marriages and Deaths*, A. & C. Black, 1972

Davenport, M., *The Book of Costume*, Crown Publishers, New York, 10 edition 1972

van Eeerde, K.S., *Wenceslas Hollar*, University Press of Virginia, 1970

Foskett, D., *British Portrait Miniatures*, Spring Books, 1963
——, *Samuel Cooper and His Contemporaries*, HMSO, 1974

Ginsburg, M., *An Introduction to Fashion Illustration*, The Compton Press and Pitman Publishing Ltd, 1980

Hind, A.M., *Engraving in England, vol. II: James I*, Cambridge University Press, 1955
——, *Hollar to Heideloff*, Costume Society, 1979

Hughes, T., *English Domestic Needlework*, Abbey Fine Arts, 1961

Jacob, J. & Simon J., *The Suffolk Collection, Catalogue of Paintings*, Greater London Council, n.d.

Laver, J., *Introduction to Costume Illustration of the Seventeenth and Eighteenth Century*, HMSO, 1951

Mactaggart, P. & A., The Rich Wearing Apparel of Richard, 3rd Earl of Dorset, *Costume Society Journal*, 1980

Mansfield, A., *Ceremonial Costume*, A. & C. Black, 1980

de Marly, D., Charles II's Own Fashion: The Theatrical Origins of the English Vest, *Journal of The Warburg & Courtauld Institutes* vol. XXXVII, 1974
——, The Establishment of Roman Dress in Seventeenth Century Portraiture, *The Burlington Magazine* vol. CXVIII, no. 868, 1975
——, The Vocabulary of the Female Head-dress 1678 – 1713, *Waffen und Kostümkunde* vol. 17, 1975
——, Fashionable Suppliers 1660 – 1700, *The Antiquaries Journal* vol. 58 pt. 2, 1978

Marshall, R., *Women in Scotland 1660 – 1780*, Scottish National Portrait Gallery, 1979

Mercer, E., *English Art 1553 – 1625*, Oxford University Press, 1962

Millar, O., *Pictures in the Royal Collection: Tudor, Stuart and Early Georgian*, Phaidon, 1963
——, *The Age of Charles I*, The Tate Gallery, 1972
Sir Peter Lely, National Portrait Gallery, 1978

Nevinson, J., *Fashion Plates and Fashion 1625 – 1635*, Apollo, vol. LI, 1950
——, The 'Mercury Gallant' or European Fashions in the 1670s, *The Connoisseur* vol. CXXVI, 1955
——, *The Origin and Early History of the Fashion Plate*, Smithsonian Press, Washington, 1969
——, Illustrations of Costume in the 'Alba Amicorum', *Archaeologia* vol. CVI, 1979

Nevinson, J. & Saunders, A., *Wenceslas Hollar: The Four Seasons*, Costume Society Extra Series, 1979

Parry, G., *Hollar's England*, Michael Russell, 1980

Piper, D., *Catalogue of Seventeenth Century Portraits in*

the National Portrait Gallery 1625 – 1714, Cambridge University Press, 1963

Reynolds, G., *Costume of the Western World: Elizabethan and Jacobean 1558 – 1625*, Harrap, 1951

Ribeiro, A., 'A Paradise of Flowers': Flowers in English Dress in the Late Sixteenth & Early Seventeenth Centuries, *The Connoisseur* vol. 202, 1979

Riddell, E., (ed.), *Lives of the Stuart Age*, Osprey, 1976

Stevenson, S. & Thomson, D., *John Michael Wright: The King's Painter*, HMSO, 1982

Strong, R., *National Portrait Gallery Tudor & Jacobean Portraits*, HMSO, 1969

——, *The English Icon*, Routledge, Kegan Paul, 1969

——, *The Elizabethan Image*, The Tate Gallery, 1969

——, Charles I's Clothes for the Years 1633 – 1635, *Costume Society Journal*, 1980

Tait, H. & Gere, C., *The Jeweller's Art*, British Museum Publications, 1979

Thornton, P., *Baroque and Rococo Silks*, Faber & Faber, 1965

Walgrave J., *De Mode in Rubens' Tijd*, Provinciaal Museum, Sterckshof, 1977

Waugh, N., *Corsets and Crinolines*, Batsford, 1954

——, *The Cut of Men's Clothes*, Faber & Faber, 1964

——, *The Cut of Women's Clothes*, Faber & Faber, 1968

Whinney, M. & Millar, O., *English Art 1626 – 1714*, Oxford University Press, 1957

Yung, K.K., *National Portrait Gallery Complete Illustrated Catalogue*, National Portrait Gallery, 1981

Glossary and Select Index

Note This lists costume and textile terms which are not fully explained elsewhere. It also gives the numbers of those illustrations showing important examples, and the earliest and latest examples of each item.

Aigrette a tuft of feathers, originally of the egret, held in place by a spray of gems. (4) (9) (23) (25)

Basque a deep, shaped band or bands of material attached below the waist of a doublet or bodice. (7) (20) (38) (57) (72)

Beaver a short-hand term meaning a hat made of expensive beaver fur. (17) (34) (39) (71) (79)

Blackwork a type of embroidery of Spanish origin, using black silk to embroider stylized or naturalistic motifs on linen or silk. (2) (3) (16)

Bombast a type of padding originally made from cotton wadding. (11)

Breeches a term applied to men's knee-length clothing. (4) (23) (85) (113) (158)

Canions the short, fitted extension sometimes worn with trunkhose (*q.v.*). (1) (4) (8)

Clocks an embroidered design on the inner and outer legs of stockings. (14) (17) (22)

Cornet a women's cap, fitting the back of the head with long lappets framing the face. (133)

Doublet one of the main male garments until c. 1670, the doublet was a type of fitted jacket with sleeves, usually buttoned at the front. (1) (25) (47) (88) (106)

Echelles a decorative arrangement of rows of ribbon bows placed in diminishing size over the front of a stomacher. (133) (146)

Falling band a turned-down collar held at the centre front by ties. (1) (4) (5)

Farthingale a hooped petticoat made from wood or, more rarely, whalebone, which gave a distinctive wheel shape to the skirt worn over it. (7) (9) (21) (43)

Fontange a high, tiered head-dress of wired lace or linen frills attached to a small linen cap worn at the back of the head. (142) (148) (158)

Frogging decorative rows of loops, buttons and braids arranged down the front of a garment. (150) (153)

Gorget a piece of armour worn to protect the throat. (1) (22) (31) (53)

Jerkin a sleeveless male garment usually worn over the doublet and similarly constructed but with a longer basque. (4) (30) (53) (73) (90)

Kerchief a square of material folded triangularly and worn round the neck and shoulders by women. (66) (72) (80)

Lappets two linen or lace streamers which were attached to the back of a woman's cap. (133) (157)

Mantua a loose gown which developed into the semi-formal fitted gown of the 1680s, held at the waist with a sash or belt. (129) (146) (158)

Nightcap a man's informal cap constructed from four conical sections of material with a turn-up border; usually of embroidered linen. (11)

Nightgown a loose fitting gown or wrap worn by women informally over a smock and petticoat. (104) (105) (113) (135)

Panes strips of material, similar to broad ribbons, caught at either end into the main construction of a sleeve, doublet or bodice. (1) (22) (40) (63) (114)

Peascod belly the distortion of the main body of a man's doublet by the addition of extra padding above the waistline. (1)

Periwig an anglicization of the French word for a man's wig, a peruke (*perruque*). (97) (102) (118) (134) (158)

Persian vest a loose man's coat held by a sash or belt and introduced by Charles II in 1666. (100)

Petticoat breeches primarily a Court fashion, of immensely wide legs pleated into a waistband but not held at the knee. (94) (106) (118)

Pickadil a standing frame with horizontal tabs, attached to the back of the doublet and used to support a ruff or standing collar. (6) (12) (38)

Pinking a decorative pattern of small holes or slits on material and leather. (3) (36) (51)

Points tagged ribbon or lace ties used to attach doublet to hose or as a decorative conceit. (8) (34) (51) (116)

Ruching a decorative form of gathering and pleating material to enhance its three-dimensional qualities. (3)

143

Ruff radiating stiffened pleats of linen or lace attached to a neckband, often constructed in multiple layers. (2) (16) (24) (39) (79)

Shag a long-haired cloth with some rough fur in its composition, used to line garments. (14)

Smock a woman's undergarment made from widths of linen in a simple T shape but often embroidered or edged with lace. (3) (39) (76) (125) (157)

Spangles small, thin pieces of metal used to decorate dress in the manner of sequins. (10) (17) (23) (40)

Steinkerk a very long cravat loosely tied, twisted casually and with its end passed through a button-hole or pinned to one side; named after a battle of 1692. (147) (156)

Stomacher a triangular, stiffened item of dress placed between the edges of an unclosed bodice and held by ties or pins. (2) (45) (61) (129) (157)

Tabs the arrangement of small sections of material around the lower edge of a doublet or bodice, also on shoulder wings, gauntlet gloves, etc.

Tippet a waist-length cape or, in the case of fur, a narrow stole or scarf.

Tricorne a man's hat cocked into an equilateral triangle with the point worn at the front of the head.

Trunkhose short, substantially padded round breeches, often worn with canions (q.v.)